Taxcafe.co.uk Tax Guides

Tax Saving Tactics for Salary Earners

Christopher Field FCCA

Important Legal Notices:

Published by:
Taxcafe UK Limited
67 Milton Road
Kirkcaldy KY1 1TL
Tel: (0044) 01592 560081
Email: team@taxcafe.co.uk

ISBN 978-1-907302-79-4

1ˢᵗ edition, September 2013

Disclaimer
Before reading or relying on the content of this tax guide please read the disclaimer.

Pay Less Tax!

...with help from Taxcafe's unique tax guides and software

All products available online at

www.taxcafe.co.uk

Popular Taxcafe titles include:

- *How to Save Property Tax*
- *Salary versus Dividends*
- *How to Save Inheritance Tax*
- *Small Business Tax Saving Tactics*
- *Tax Saving Tactics for Salary Earners*
- *Using a Property Company to Save Tax*
- *Property Capital Gains Tax*
- *Using a Company to Save Tax*
- *Keeping it Simple: Small Business Bookkeeping, Tax & VAT*
- *Non-Resident & Offshore Tax Planning*
- *The World's Best Tax Havens*
- *Tax Saving Tactics for Non-Doms*
- *Isle of Man Tax Saving Guide*
- *Capital Allowances*
- *Tax Saving Tactics for Motorists*
- *How to Protect Your Child Benefit*

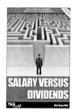

Disclaimer

- This guide is intended as **general guidance** only and does NOT constitute accountancy, tax, investment or other professional advice.

- The author and Taxcafe UK Limited make no representations or warranties with respect to the accuracy or completeness of this publication and cannot accept any responsibility or liability for any loss or risk, personal or otherwise, which may arise, directly or indirectly, from reliance on information contained in this publication.

- Please note that tax legislation, the law and practices of Government and regulatory authorities (e.g. HM Revenue & Customs) are constantly changing. We therefore recommend that for accountancy, tax, investment or other professional advice, you consult a suitably qualified accountant, tax advisor, financial adviser, or other professional adviser.

- Please also note that your personal circumstances may vary from the general examples provided in this guide and your professional adviser will be able to provide specific advice based on your personal circumstances.

- This guide covers UK taxation only and any references to 'tax' or 'taxation', unless the contrary is expressly stated, refer to UK taxation only. Please note that references to the 'UK' do not include the Channel Islands or the Isle of Man. Foreign tax implications are beyond the scope of this guide.

- All persons described in the examples in this guide are entirely fictional. Any similarities to actual persons, living or dead, or to fictional characters created by any other author, are entirely coincidental.

About the Author

Christopher Field FCCA is a Chartered Certified Accountant practising in Purley Oaks, Surrey. He qualified in 1988 and spent the early part of his career in financial services before setting up on his own with Acumen Accounting in 2000. He specialises in tax planning and compliance work for small companies and has built a strong local reputation.

When he is not helping his clients with their accounts and tax returns, Chris enjoys writing articles, busying himself around the house and spending time with his friends and family. His future plans include writing more books, expanding his business and touring the world with his wife, Svetlana.

Contents

Introduction

This book is aimed at the vast majority of people who have a steady job, earn a regular wage or salary and pay tax under PAYE.

Most tax books, by contrast, are aimed at business owners or wealthy individuals. After all, they're the ones with the most freedom to control their tax affairs, aren't they?

Tax is something that just seems to *happen* to the vast majority of salary earners. However, as it happens, salary earners *can* do a surprising amount of lucrative tax planning, as you will discover in the chapters that follow.

This book shows you how to make your income as tax efficient as possible, using a whole array of allowances and exemptions which most people are totally unaware of.

In short, it will help you maximise your take-home pay.

Part 1 contains a plain-English guide to *how* salary earners are taxed and a useful table showing all the income tax and national insurance paid at different salary levels.

You'll discover why your tax code might be wrong and why this may mean you're paying too much tax or too little tax.

Part 2 covers *tax-free* benefits-in-kind. You may be pleasantly surprised by the ones that are still available and added together the tax savings could run to thousands of pounds.

They include:

- Childcare
- Mobile phones
- Parking
- Computers
- Work canteens
- Business trips and holidays
- Cheap loans
- Long-service awards
- Staff suggestion schemes
- Gyms and sports facilities

1

- Relocation expenses
- Eye tests and health care
- Staff parties
- Bicycles
- Redundancy training
- Life insurance
- Gifts and entertainment

In Part 3 we move on to salary sacrifice schemes (swapping salary for tax-free benefits). These can save you both income tax and *national insurance*. In many cases you can also enjoy your employer's national insurance saving.

You'll discover how to increase your pension fund by up to 34% with a salary sacrifice pension, how to save up to £1,866 per year with childcare vouchers and how to save £961 per year with a company car.

Part 4 is all about tax-free expenses – expenses that your employer can reimburse tax-free or you can claim directly on your tax return, including:

- Travel expenses
- Subsistence
- Hotels
- Entertaining
- Working from home

This book will show just how far you can push the boat out, with your employer's permission of course.

Child benefit is extremely valuable (worth £1,752 per year if you have two children and £2,449 if you have three children). In Part 5 you will find out how to avoid the new child benefit charge by making pension contributions (with tax relief of up to 77%).

You can also protect your child benefit with childcare vouchers, by deferring income and reducing your working hours (it is actually possible to work less and have more income!).

Contractors & Personal Service Companies

This book covers personal service companies in tremendous detail.

Temporary staff often work through their own companies but in all other respects are just "wage slaves" like their colleagues – without the employment rights and benefits that the latter take for granted.

In certain circumstances using a company can save you national insurance and in one case study we show how a contractor saves over £4,700 per year. A company can also help you split your income with your spouse or partner. In one example we show how doing this could save you an extra £10,673 per year.

However, these tax savings are by no means guaranteed – getting it wrong could be financially disastrous. Most contractors with their own companies are acutely aware of the so-called 'IR35' tax rules, without really knowing for sure whether they're affected or what they can do. This book explains exactly how the IR35 rules work and what you can do about them.

Staff Share Schemes

Part 7 covers staff share schemes. These offer lots of benefits. For example, some schemes allow you to take tax-free shares instead of taxable salary. They also offer capital gains tax benefits. The guide covers all the main schemes including:

- Share Incentive Plans (SIPs)
- Save as You Earn (SAYE)
- Enterprise Management Incentives
- Company Share Option Plans

We cover all the latest changes to these schemes and show exactly how much tax you could potentially save.

Some salary earners also have part-time businesses and in Part 8 we explain all the tax rules, including how to offset losses against your other income (including your salary) and all the expenses you can claim, including wages paid to your spouse/partner or children, travel expenses, home expenses and interest on borrowings.

Part 9 covers two important domestic tax matters in detail: hiring a nanny and taking on a lodger. If you employ a nanny you are responsible for paying her tax and national insurance, so it is vital to get it right. For lodgers, we examine the rent-a-room scheme in sufficient detail for you to decide whether it is worthwhile.

Finally, we end with a Bonus Chapter covering a whole bunch of important future tax changes. The most important of these is the Government's new childcare vouchers scheme. Will this be better than your employer's existing childcare scheme? Our examples show you when it will be and when it won't.

I hope you enjoy this book and find at least something that helps you keep a bit more of your hard-earned income. After all, you deserve it! Remember it was you who earned it in the first place, not the State, which seems to grab an ever-increasing share!

Good luck.

Part 1

Salary Earners: Tax Basics

Chapter 1

How Much Tax Do Salary Earners Pay?

Calculating Your Income Tax

For the 2013/14 tax year, starting on 6th April 2013, most individuals pay income tax as follows on their salaries:

- 0%   first   £9,440   (personal allowance)
- 20%   next   £32,010   (basic-rate band)
- 40%   above   £41,450   (higher-rate threshold)

Generally speaking, if you earn more than £41,450 you are a *higher-rate taxpayer*. If you earn less you are a *basic-rate taxpayer*.

Example – Basic-Rate Taxpayer

John earns a salary of £30,000. His income tax for 2013/14 can be calculated as follows:

- *0% on the first £9,440 = £0*
- *20% on the next £20,560 = £4,112*

Total income tax bill: £4,112

Example – Higher-Rate Taxpayer

Jane earns a salary of £60,000. Her income tax for 2013/14 is:

- *0% on the first £9,440 = £0*
- *20% on the next £32,010 = £6,402*
- *40% on the final £18,550 = £7,420*

Total income tax bill: £13,822

Income over £100,000

When your taxable income exceeds £100,000 your income tax personal allowance is gradually withdrawn. For every additional £1 you earn, 50p of your personal allowance is taken away.

What this means is that, when your income reaches £118,880, your personal allowance will have completely disappeared.

It also means that those who earn a salary of between £100,000 and £118,880 face a marginal income tax rate of 60%.

Example

Caroline has received salary income of £100,000 so far during the current tax year.

If she receives an extra £1,000 of income she will pay an extra £400 of income tax. She will also lose £500 of her income tax personal allowance, so £500 of previously tax-free salary will now be taxed at 40%, adding £200 to her tax bill.

All in all, she pays £600 in tax on her extra £1,000 of income, so her marginal income tax rate is 60%.

Income above £150,000

Once your taxable income exceeds £150,000, you pay 45% income tax on any extra salary you receive.

This is known as the additional rate of tax. It fell from 50% to 45% at the start of the 2013/14 tax year.

If you earn less than £100,000 or £150,000 it's worth pointing out that those thresholds have not increased with inflation since they were introduced several years ago.

This means more and more taxpayers are likely to be dragged into these higher tax brackets over time.

Calculating Your National Insurance

For the current 2013/14 tax year most individuals pay national insurance as follows on salary income:

- 0%   on the first   £7,755   (earnings threshold)
- 12% on the next   £33,695
- 2%   above   £41,450 (upper earnings limit)

Example – Basic-Rate Taxpayer

John earns a salary of £30,000. His national insurance for 2013/14 is:

- *0%   on the first   £7,755   = £0*
- *12% on the next   £22,245 = £2,669*

John's national insurance bill: £2,669

Example – Higher-Rate Taxpayer

Jane earns a salary of £60,000. Her national insurance for 2013/14 is:

- *0%   on the first   £7,755   = £0*
- *12% on the next   £33,695 = £4,043*
- *2%   on the final £18,550 = £371*

Jane's national insurance bill: £4,414

Combined Tax Rates

The combined marginal rates of income tax and national insurance applying to salaries in 2013/14 are as follows:

Income up to £7,755	0%
Income from £7,755 to £9,440	12%
Income from £9,440 to £41,450	32%
Income from £41,450 to £100,000	42%
Income from £100,000 to £118,880	62%
Income from £118,880 to £150,000	42%
Income over £150,000	47%

Employer's National Insurance

Employers pay 13.8% national insurance on every single pound the employee earns over £7,696. There is no cap.

You probably don't lose much sleep over your employer's national insurance bill. However, employer's national insurance is a tax on YOUR income. If it didn't exist your employer would be able to pay you a higher salary.

Example

Jane's employer pays national insurance on her £60,000 salary as follows:

- *0%   on the first   £7,696   = £0*
- *13.8%   on the next £52,304 = £7,218*

Jane's employer's national insurance bill: £7,218

Tax Bills Combined

John and Jane's total tax bills can be summarised as follows:

John – Basic-rate Taxpayer – £30,000

	£
Income tax	4,112
Employee's national insurance	2,669
Employer's national insurance	3,078
Total taxes	**9,859**

Jane – Higher-rate Taxpayer – £60,000

	£
Income tax	13,822
Employee's national insurance	4,414
Employer's national insurance	7,218
Total taxes	**25,454**

TABLE 1
Total Tax Paid by Salary Earners 2013/14

Salary	Income Tax	National Insurance	Total	%	Employer's NI	%
10,000	£112	£269	381	4	318	7
20,000	£2,112	£1,469	3,581	18	1,698	26
30,000	£4,112	£2,669	6,781	23	3,078	33
40,000	£6,112	£3,869	9,981	25	4,458	36
50,000	£9,822	£4,214	14,036	28	5,838	40
60,000	£13,822	£4,414	18,236	30	7,218	42
70,000	£17,822	£4,614	22,436	32	8,598	44
80,000	£21,822	£4,814	26,636	33	9,978	46
90,000	£25,822	£5,014	30,836	34	11,358	47
100,000	£29,822	£5,214	35,036	35	12,738	48
110,000	£35,822	£5,414	41,236	37	14,118	50
120,000	£41,598	£5,614	47,212	39	15,498	52
130,000	£45,598	£5,814	51,412	40	16,878	53
140,000	£49,598	£6,014	55,612	40	18,258	53
150,000	£53,598	£6,214	59,812	40	19,638	53
160,000	£58,098	£6,414	64,512	40	21,018	53
170,000	£62,598	£6,614	69,212	41	22,398	54
180,000	£67,098	£6,814	73,912	41	23,778	54
190,000	£71,598	£7,014	78,612	41	25,158	55
200,000	£76,098	£7,214	83,312	42	26,538	55

When you include employer's national insurance it's startling how much tax is paid even by those on relatively modest incomes. Direct taxes on John's income come to 33%.

Jane's £60,000 salary is not low by any standards but you wouldn't describe her as a high income earner either. Nevertheless an amount equivalent to 42% of her salary is paid in direct taxes on her income.

Table 1 shows the total income tax and national insurance paid at other salary levels. The first '%' column is the salary earner's overall effective tax rate. For example, if you earn £40,000, income tax and national insurance will eat up 25% of your salary.

The second '%' column adds in employer's national insurance. For example, if you earn £40,000, an amount equivalent to 36% of your income is paid in taxes.

Future Income Tax Changes

In the March 2013 Budget, it was announced that income tax will be levied as follows in the next 2014/15 tax year:

- 0%   on the first   £10,000   Personal allowance
- 20%   on the next   £31,865   Basic-rate band
- 40%   above   £41,865   Higher-rate threshold

The personal allowance will continue to be withdrawn when your income exceeds £100,000 and will be completely taken away if your income exceeds £120,000.

No changes have been announced to the 45% additional rate that applies to income over £150,000.

Chapter 2

How the Tax System Works

HM Revenue & Customs (HMRC) is the authority in charge of the UK tax system. It is responsible for income tax, national insurance, VAT, stamp duty and all the other taxes, as well as the tax credit system.

This book is concerned mainly with employment taxes – income tax and national insurance. These are the main taxes that salary earners pay. Capital gains tax also gets a brief mention in places.

There are two systems for dealing with income tax and national insurance:

- PAYE (Pay as You Earn)
- Self assessment (submitting a tax return)

PAYE is compulsory for employees whilst self assessment is mainly for the self-employed. However, there are some employees who also submit tax returns.

PAYE

The PAYE system was introduced in 1948 and makes it compulsory for your employer to deduct income tax and national insurance from your earnings where appropriate. All such deductions must be shown on your pay slip.

Income tax deductions are calculated using tax codes. Your tax code tells your employer how much tax-free income you're entitled to during the tax year and therefore how much tax to deduct before they pay you.

Chapter 3 deals with tax codes in more detail. These allow your tax affairs to be dealt with by your employer without the need to complete a tax return or pay any tax to HMRC directly.

Under PAYE, income tax is usually based on your total earnings to date for the current tax year. This means that if you are "between jobs" your tax position will "catch up" when you start working again. The amount of tax deducted will go down for a while when you start a new job after a period of unemployment.

If your employment terminates before the end of the tax year and you do not start a new job until the next tax year, you will normally be due a tax rebate. You will have to apply to HMRC for this at the end of the tax year and supply a copy of your P45.

If you have more than one job, your second employer will probably deduct tax at a flat 20%. This ensures that you do not get the benefit of two personal allowances.

National Insurance

National insurance is also deducted under PAYE but is calculated separately from income tax and is not based on your tax code. It is always based on your earnings for the current week/month, not the year to date (unless you are a director, in which case it is based on your earnings for the year to date).

Thus, if you have any breaks in your employment during the year, there is no reduction in your national insurance deductions when you start working again. Nor can you apply for a rebate at the end of the tax year.

However, you do get the benefit of two national insurance free thresholds if you have more than one job at the same time, provided the employers are totally separate. For 2013/14 the threshold is £7,755, so if you have two jobs you can potentially earn up to £15,510 before national insurance kicks in.

If your combined earnings from different jobs exceed the upper earnings limit (£41,450 for 2013/14) you may end up paying too much national insurance. In that case, you can apply to HMRC for a rebate at the end of the tax year.

Self-Assessment

People on self-assessment must complete a tax return once a year and pay some or all of their tax to HMRC directly. They have a 10 digit UTR number in addition to their national insurance number and receive annual statements from HMRC.

Some employees may be on self-assessment as well as PAYE. This usually happens when they:

- Are company directors
- Have a part-time business
- Have more than one job
- Have a pension as well as a job
- Receive substantial investment income
- Have rental properties
- Have untaxed income from any other source
- Claim child benefit and earn more than £50,000
- Owe capital gains tax on the disposal of investments
- Have recently become UK tax resident

If most of your income comes from employment and is taxed under PAYE, it is unlikely that you will have to pay tax on your other income directly to HMRC. Instead, HMRC will usually adjust your tax code and collect the tax via PAYE.

However, if your tax bill is more than £3,000 or you did not file your tax return by 31st December following the end of the tax year, HMRC will not adjust your tax code in this way. You will have to pay the tax directly by 31st January instead.

Payments on Account

If the tax you owe is more than £3,000 and more than 20% of your total tax liability for the year, you will have to start paying tax twice a year under the payments-on-account regime. This is unusual for employees but does happen in rare cases.

This means you will have to pay *estimated* tax bills on 31st January and 31st July based on what you owed for the previous tax year. If the actual tax bill for the year turns out to be higher, you must pay the balance owing by the following 31st January.

For example, if your tax liability for 2012/13 was £20,000 but you only paid £15,000 under PAYE, you must pay the balance of £5,000 by 31st January 2014. You must also pay £2,500 by this date as a payment on account for 2013/14, followed by a further £2,500 on or before 31st July 2014.

If your tax liability for 2013/14 turns out to be less than your payments on account, you can ask HMRC for a tax rebate, plus interest. You can do this online by logging in to your HMRC account and entering your bank details.

However, if your *actual* tax liability for 2013/14 is, say, £22,000 and you paid £16,000 under PAYE, then you will still have to pay £1,000 by 31st January 2015 (£22,000 - £16,000 - £5,000 payments on account).

You will not be charged interest on the outstanding tax as long as you paid the automatically calculated payments on account based on the previous year's tax.

Sometimes, you may expect your untaxed income to be a lot less this year than last year, for example if you received a large one-off income payment or your rental profits fall because of large maintenance bills. In that case, you may apply for your payments on account to be reduced.

Bear in mind though that if you are wrong and your tax bill does not go down, you will have to pay HMRC interest based on the difference between what your payments on account should have been and what you reduced them to.

Tax returns, registering for self-assessment and HMRC penalties are discussed more fully in Part 8: Running a Part-time Business.

Chapter 3

Checking Your Tax Code

Most people are familiar with the green *PAYE Coding Notice* they get from HM Revenue & Customs each year, telling them which tax code their employers should use to calculate their PAYE deductions.

If you are lucky, it is the only letter you will ever get from HMRC, as it indicates that all your tax affairs can be dealt with by your employer from that one short code, without the need for you to complete a tax return or pay any taxes to HMRC direct.

Yet how many people actually understand how their tax code is calculated, and know whether it is right or not? What do all those adjustments mean, like reductions to collect unpaid tax or higher-rate income restrictions? More to the point, are they correct? This is where you have to look at your tax code in a bit more detail and contact HMRC if you think they have made a mistake.

What is a Tax Code?

A tax code is designed to allow your employer to deduct the correct amount of tax through the PAYE system. It usually consists of three numbers and a letter that determine your "free pay" for that week or month. This is pay that you will not be taxed on.

For example, the code 944L tells your employer to allow "free pay" of £787.42 per month, which is equivalent to £9,449 per year. They can look up these "free pay" figures in tax tables published by HMRC, although it is usually all done by software these days. Your remaining pay is then taxed at 20%, 40% or 45% (or a combination of these rates) depending on your income. Tax codes are never used to work out national insurance contributions. These are based on a different system.

If your tax affairs are very simple, the only item in your code will be your personal allowance. For 2013/14 this is £9,440 so your code will be 944L. In fact, you probably won't even get a PAYE Coding Notice if your tax code is as simple as that.

Who Needs a Tax Code?

You should receive a PAYE coding notice if you:

- Receive benefits-in-kind, such as a company car
- Are a higher-rate taxpayer and get investment income
- Have more than one job
- Receive a pension as well as employment income
- Receive untaxed income from other sources
- Have claimed too much in tax credits
- Have to pay tax on child benefit
- Earn more than £100,000 a year
- Make regular pension contributions
- Are able to claim other allowances
- Owe tax from previous years
- Claim allowable expenses for doing your job

In most of these cases, you will be in the self-assessment system and required to complete a tax return every year. However, this is not always the case, and it is people who do not have to file a tax return who are most at risk from incorrect tax codes.

Why Might My Tax Code Be Wrong?

Usually it's because HMRC don't have up-to-date information. The following are the more common reasons for incorrect tax codes:

- The wrong information has been entered on a P11D
- There is untaxed income which has never been reported
- Employers or pension providers used the wrong tax code
- HMRC estimated too much bank interest
- You or your partner claim taxable child benefit
- You no longer live with someone claiming child benefit
- You became entitled to age allowances
- Your income exceeded the threshold for age allowances
- You have not claimed losses on a new business
- You have not claimed allowances such as gift aid
- You paid outstanding tax after your code was adjusted for it
- Your investment income takes you into higher-rate tax

A few of these may be corrected eventually – but most won't.

When Your Tax Code Might be Corrected

Tax code errors are normally corrected automatically when either:

- You file a tax return each year, or

- The error is just a timing difference between tax years

The latter situation is common with P11Ds, where a benefit-in-kind may be taxed using last year's figure. Company cars are a very good example. The tax on these goes up every year if you keep the same car, so the figure in your tax code will always be out of date.

This is not really an error – you are simply getting extra time to pay the tax on last year's benefit. The tax system will catch up later when the P11D for the current year is filed.

If you are in the self-assessment system, any errors in your code will be corrected when you file your tax return. By filing online, you will see your total tax liability for the year less the tax deducted under PAYE and on your investment income.

If your tax code was wrong for some reason, the tax figure on your annual *P60 End of Year Certificate* will be too high or too low and this will be corrected through a tax payment or a tax refund to/from HMRC. In other words, it will all come out in the wash.

However, if you are not in the self-assessment system and tax code errors are not adjusted each year, the tax underpayment or overpayment could become permanent, or at the very least not spotted by HMRC for many years.

When Your Tax Code Might <u>Not</u> Be Corrected

This typically happens when HMRC lacks information altogether and you need to inform them. Usually this is when your personal circumstances have changed in some way.

As a taxpayer, it is your responsibility to tell HMRC whenever you receive a new source of untaxed income. Becoming self-employed or renting out a house are obvious examples. You should never wait for the taxman to spot these first, as you may have to pay late notification penalties, plus interest on any late tax.

The same goes for anything on which you can claim tax relief. You only have four years to report losses or allowances or you may lose them altogether.

There are certain things you can assume that HMRC will know about. For example, they will be aware of your pension contributions as you have to give the pension firm your national insurance number. The same goes for benefits-in-kind, as your employer must report these on a P11D.

Other situations are not so obvious, such as investment income. Normally you do not need to report investment income, such as bank interest and dividends, as they are deemed to be paid net of basic-rate tax (unless you applied for interest to be paid gross at some time).

However, once you become a higher-rate taxpayer, you should be paying more tax on your investment income. You could easily become one without even knowing it. For example, your salary could all be taxed at the basic rate but your investment income might take you over the higher-rate threshold.

The new child benefit charge is also likely to cause confusion. The tax system does not know who is living with whom, so if one of you has "adjusted net income" in excess of £50,000 you will need to inform HMRC. This is bound to drag many more people into the self-assessment system.

There could well be situations where HMRC is aware of your circumstances but still gets your tax code wrong due to incorrect information being held in their systems. You need to tell them otherwise the error may never be corrected.

The most common such situations are as follows:

P11D Benefits and Expenses

P11D is the form that employers give to employees and submit to HMRC, reporting benefits-in-kind and expense payments that have not been put through the payroll.

Sometimes P11Ds are wrong because the benefit-in-kind has been valued incorrectly. These mistakes are unlikely to be picked up unless you know how to calculate the figures. Again, company cars are a classic example. They are very easy for employers to get wrong, especially as the tax tends to change every year.

Expenses also sometimes need to be reported on a P11D. Most large employers have a dispensation to avoid reporting them if they are not taxable, but smaller employers may not have applied for one and suddenly find that they are obliged to report them.

In that case, the expenses are likely to turn up in your tax code, especially the ones that are not travel and subsistence, and you will find yourself being taxed on them unless you tell HMRC that they were all incurred in the course of your duties.

You can do that on a tax return by entering the expenses first under *Benefits from your employment* and then as *Employment expenses* – this way they cancel each other out. Alternatively, you can write to HMRC instead. This is known as a section 336 claim.

Restrictions to Personal Allowances

Since April 2010, the tax-free personal allowance has been restricted if your "adjusted net income" for the year exceeds £100,000. This means you lose £1 of your personal allowance for every £2 of income above the £100,000 threshold.

HMRC adjusts your tax code for this in the expectation that the same thing will happen the following year. They use your income from last year as a guide and reduce your tax code accordingly. Any difference is then coded out or refunded the following year.

However, some people only go over the £100,000 threshold thanks to a one-off event such as a bonus, a golden handshake or a gain on a non-qualifying life policy. Therefore, no restriction is due for the current year and your tax code should not be adjusted.

Such errors are likely to be corrected in due course, but meanwhile you will experience a significant drop in your net salary, so it is always best to write and ask for your tax code to be corrected.

Coding-out Adjustments

These are another rich source of HMRC errors. They occur where you owe some tax for a previous year and your tax code is adjusted accordingly. Then you go and pay the tax anyway, so the tax ends up being paid twice.

You can stop HMRC doing this by ticking a box on your tax return, but then you only have until 31st January following the end of the tax year to pay up, so you might prefer to have your tax code adjusted instead. That way you get a whole year to pay the amount outstanding.

However, you then need to report the tax code adjustment on your next tax return, so it can get a bit messy. If you don't, it will look like you have paid too much tax, causing an error in the outstanding balance. Fortunately, most such errors are picked up by the HMRC systems, which then send a corrected statement.

People making payments on account twice a year can also fall foul of coding-out adjustments. Bi-annual payments are normally only due from the self-employed, but employees with substantial investment income may also have to make them.

Normally you only fall into the payments-on-account regime if your outstanding tax for the previous year was more than 20% of your total tax liability. It is not unknown for HMRC to adjust your tax code even though you are paying twice a year on account.

Finally, bear in mind that HMRC can only "code out" tax bills if they are less than £3,000. Otherwise, you have to pay them in one go by 31st January following the year of assessment.

Pensioners

HMRC often gets pensioners tax codes wrong. Possibly this is because very few of them are on self-assessment, so errors are not picked up from tax returns. Consequently, when errors do occur, they tend to be perpetuated from one year to the next.

A common scenario is the following: a woman starts getting a widow's pension following the death of her husband. The pension provider may not have information about her other pensions and uses the wrong tax code for her monthly payment. As a result she may not pay enough tax on her widow's pension and, because she does not file tax returns, the underpayment may not be revealed for several years. The pension provider files year end returns but the fact they are using the wrong tax code does not get picked up due to deficiencies in HMRC systems.

Now that HMRC has improved its systems, many such cases are coming out of the woodwork and triggering tax demands for prior years. Fortunately, many pensioners can ask for such arrears to be wiped out under Extra Statutory Concession A19.

This can be allowed on the grounds that the taxpayer was unaware there were any arrears and did not give false or misleading information. It is also possible for the pension provider to be made responsible for the arrears if the mistake was at their end.

Employment Expenses

There are very few expenses that employees can claim against tax, and any they do incur tend to be reimbursed by the employer, so they tend not to feature in tax code notices very often. The main exception is professional subscriptions to recognised bodies.

Many employers pay these on behalf of their staff, and in that case they should not appear on your coding notice at all. However, if you pay them yourself, you should claim them against tax.

Trouble is, unless you file a tax return each year, HMRC will not know the latest subscription and the adjustment to your tax code will be based on an old figure. In that case, you will need to write to your tax office and ask them to change it.

Some expenses are tax free if your employer reimburses you but not if they don't. The scale rates for incidental overnight expenses on business trips are a good example. These cannot be claimed as a deduction on your tax return.

However, you can claim business mileage of up to 45p per mile tax free even if your employer does not pay you that much. Suppose you only get 25p per mile from your employer. You are allowed to claim the other 20p per mile on your tax return.

However, the tax-free rate drops to 25p after 10,000 miles per annum, so if your employer pays you a flat rate 30p for <u>all</u> mileage, you will have to declare the extra 5p above 10,000 miles.

You can also claim capital allowances for equipment used in your job even if your employer does not reimburse you, but they must be for items you *have* to buy. For example, you cannot claim for a computer if you have a perfectly good one at work.

You cannot claim for things like clothes, haircuts, or household expenses, even if you work at home or consider them necessary for your job in order to be suitably presentable. This is because there is a dual purpose. They are not wholly for work purposes.

Any tax-deductible expenses not reimbursed by your employer should appear on your coding notice as a credit item. If they do not, or the figures are wrong, you should tell your tax office.

Wrong Estimates

If you are a higher-rate taxpayer, HMRC sometimes estimates your taxable investment income (non-ISA bank interest, dividends, etc) and adjusts your tax code downwards, so you pay the tax under PAYE. Usually they use the same figure every year.

If you are not in the self-assessment system, you will never get a chance to correct this on a tax return. With low interest rates over the last few years, many of these estimates are far too high and result in tax being paid on income that was never received.

You now only have four years from the end of the tax year to notify HMRC of these errors and claim a tax rebate. Otherwise you will lose the rebate for good.

Getting a Tax Code Corrected

You will probably need to complete a Short Tax Return to correct the sort of mistakes mentioned above and claim what's owing to you. To get one of these, you can either write to HMRC at the address on the coding notice or call the 0300 number shown. However, be prepared for a long wait and an arduous slog through the automated switchboard.

Unfortunately, your employer cannot help much here as they have nothing to do with the coding notices and must use the tax code they are given whether it is right or wrong. All they can do is offer advice on how to approach HMRC and get it corrected.

Part 2

Tax-Free Benefits-in-Kind

Chapter 4

General Points about Benefits

Anyone who receives an annual P11D from their employer knows only too well that most benefits-in-kind are certainly not tax-free. The general rule is that you are taxed on either the cost to your employer or the market value of the benefit (although there are special rules for certain types of benefit such as company cars/vans and residential accommodation).

However, there are still some employment benefits that are either completely tax-free or offer some significant tax and/or national insurance savings. These are vitally important to anyone who is serious about maximising the tax efficiency of their remuneration package.

Even if you cannot get these benefits from your employer as a perk it may still be advantageous to negotiate them as part of a salary sacrifice deal. This procedure is fully described in Part 3.

It should be noted, for what it's worth, that only employees earning *at a rate of* at least £8,500 per annum (including the value of taxable benefits) are actually taxed on most benefits-in-kind. This is a pro-rata threshold so if you work for an employer for less than one complete tax year it is reduced for the weeks/months that you did not work.

Employees earning less than £8,500 (apart from full-time directors with a material interest in their companies) get most benefits from their employers tax-free (except for those that must be reported by employers on Form P9D).

This threshold has been frozen for over 30 years now so very few people still qualify. You would need to be a part-time worker even if you were only earning the national minimum wage.

The most important employment benefits (in terms of both tax efficiency and financial reward) are undoubtedly pensions and approved share option schemes. These are fully described in Chapter 27 and Part 7 respectively, so we shall concentrate on the less well known benefits in this chapter.

Chapter 5

Childcare

There are three ways in which employers can provide tax-free childcare to their staff:

- Workplace nurseries
- Directly contracted childcare
- Childcare vouchers

Workplace nursery facilities such as crèches or play-groups are totally tax-free. It does not matter how much the employer pays for them, the employee will not be taxed on a benefit-in-kind.

However, the employer must provide the premises for the nursery (either alone or jointly with another employer) and must be wholly or partly responsible for managing and financing it.

For childcare vouchers or directly contracted childcare, there is a tax-free limit of £55 per week (or £243 per month). However, this limit only applies if you are a basic-rate taxpayer or if you joined your employer's childcare scheme by 5th April 2011.

For higher-rate taxpayers who joined their employer's childcare scheme *after* this date, the tax-free limit is £28 per week (or £124 per month).

For additional rate taxpayers (those with incomes above £150,000 per annum) the tax-free limit is only £25 per week (or £110 per month).

Any childcare benefits in excess of these limits will be taxed, so if you become a higher-rate taxpayer this year you will lose part of the tax-free benefit next year and find a new item on your annual P11D (unless you were already in the scheme on 5th April 2011).

The tax-free childcare exemption is per **employee**, not per child. You could be the old woman who lived in a shoe and you would still only get a maximum of £55 per week.

However, both parents qualify for their own exemption, so a family could benefit from double the tax-free rate if both parents are entitled, even if they work for the same employer.

You qualify for the exemption from the day your child is born. It also applies to stepchildren or any other child for whom you have parental responsibility (such as adopted children or foster children). The exemption lasts right up to 1st September after your child's 15th birthday (or the 16th if he/she is disabled).

All three types of childcare must be made available by the employer to all eligible staff in order to be tax free. It cannot be reserved as a perk for selected individuals otherwise it will be taxable.

However, an employer can place a limit on the number of children given places in a workplace nursery, as long as it does not discriminate unfairly against particular employees (indeed the employer would have to do this in order to comply with health and safety rules).

Voucher Benefits

Some employers prefer to contract directly with approved childcare providers rather than set up a vouchers scheme. However, vouchers do have several advantages:

- They can be used for different childcare providers, so no need to inform your employer if you start using a different nursery.

- There is no statutory time limit on vouchers (although there may be expiry dates set by the scheme), so they can be saved up from the moment the child is born and redeemed whenever you wish until the child ceases to qualify.

- Unused childcare vouchers can be replaced with new ones if they do expire (provided the child continues to qualify).

- You can use them for any qualifying child whereas employer contracts may refer to one specific child.

- Childcare vouchers remain valid even after you cease working for that employer (subject to the rules of the scheme).

- You can use childcare vouchers for any qualifying purpose, which includes any extra-curricular activity where the carer needs to be registered with OFSTED (or approved in some other way). This can include summer camps, ballet lessons, music classes, horse-riding, tennis coaching, etc.

- Some of the larger voucher companies offer a range of family discounts such as shopping vouchers, leisure attractions, special offers and childcare activities.

How Much Tax You Save

At £243 per month you could receive childcare vouchers worth a total of £2,916 per annum – double that if both parents get them. The tax saving depends on whether your employer gives this to you for "free" or whether it is part of a salary sacrifice scheme.

Salary sacrifice is dealt with in Part 3 so we will not consider it any further here. Let's just assume that the childcare is a "free" perk. A basic-rate taxpayer would have to earn £4,288 in order to pay for childcare worth £2,916 out of taxed income.

Therefore, he is saving tax and national insurance of £1,372 per annum at current rates.

Higher-rate taxpayers do even better (assuming they joined a scheme by 5th April 2011 and get the maximum £243 per month). They would have to earn £5,027 to pay for £2,916 out of taxed income. That's a saving of £2,111 per annum.

Even higher-rate taxpayers who only get childcare worth £124 per month still manage to save tax and national insurance of £1,077 per annum, whilst 45% taxpayers on £110 per month save £1,170.

Chapter 6

Mobile Phones

Not many people remember Norman Lamont's infamous tax on mobile phones. It was in the 1991 Budget, when Lamont slapped a £200 flat rate charge on the private use of mobile phones provided by employers.

He called them "one of the greatest scourges of modern life" and hoped that "as a result of this measure, restaurants will be quieter".

Of course, it made no difference to mobile phone use and simply imposed an additional burden on employers who had to identify which phones had been used for private calls or treat them all as taxable benefits. The tax was finally scrapped in 1999.

Since then mobile phones have been tax-free. You can now run up bills of thousands of pounds for private calls at your employer's expense and pay no tax on them at all. However, there are some conditions you must obey in order to qualify for this exemption:

- The mobile phone contract must be in the employer's name. The exemption does not apply to contracts in the employee's name. In fact, employees cannot even claim a proportion of their mobile phone bills as expenses for business use, as the tariff is usually the same no matter how many calls they make. They can only claim for itemised business calls.

- An employee can only benefit from this exemption on **one** mobile phone. Any others will be taxed unless the phone was provided for business use and private use was "not significant".

- PDAs and other such advanced gadgets that combine the functions of a mobile phone with those of a computer *may* not qualify for the exemption, although they are exempt anyway if private use is "not significant". However, HMRC now concede that BlackBerries, iPhones and other smartphones qualify for the tax-free exemption in their own right.

- The mobile phone must be provided by the employer. This effectively means the handset must belong to the employer.

- A mobile phone provided to a member of an employee's family or household does not qualify for the exemption unless that individual is also an employee in their own right.

These conditions are fairly easy to comply with and should present no problems for the average employee.

How Much Tax You Save

This depends on your monthly bills but assuming an average of £30 per month, a basic-rate taxpayer would have to earn an extra £529 a year to cover that cost out of taxed income.

He would save tax and national insurance of £169 per year on that extra salary, whilst a higher-rate taxpayer would save £260 per year and an additional rate taxpayer £319 per year.

Of course, your employer may place a limit on the size of bill you can actually rack up.

Chapter 7

Workplace Parking

If you use your car, motorbike or bicycle to commute to work and park "at or near" your normal place of work, your employer can pay the parking costs, including annual permits, and you will pay no tax on the benefit whatsoever.

Your employer can also provide you with a free parking space without any taxable benefit arising.

This could be a huge benefit given the cost of parking now in most towns and cities. For example, an annual season ticket for a car park in central London could cost over £5,000. This benefit would save a higher-rate taxpayer £2,100 a year in tax and national insurance.

The phrase "at or near" is not defined in the legislation and can be interpreted fairly widely. For example, you could use an annual permit to park your car anywhere within the permitted zone without a taxable benefit arising.

However, there must not be any dual purpose. In other words, you cannot receive a tax-free benefit for workplace parking if you live at or near your place of work and do not even bother to drive in.

Parking has got to be mainly for work purposes in order for the exemption to apply.

Parking costs can be either paid directly by the employer or reimbursed to the employee as out-of-pocket expenses. In the latter case, it would be wise for the employee to furnish receipts and state exactly where the car was parked to avoid any queries.

A word of warning though. Local authorities are now permitted to impose a Workplace Parking Levy on businesses that allow their staff to park on-site, and many have plans to do so.

These levies are expected to be around £300 a year for each parking space.

The levy is chargeable on the employer, not on employees. However, many employers may pass the charge on to their staff and even add VAT as they will be making a taxable supply.

Fortunately the council levy only applies to on-site parking, not to public roads or external car parks. Therefore, it should not affect the vast majority of employers who do not have the space to allow more than a few of their staff to park on-site anyway.

Chapter 8

Computers

A few years ago there was a very handy tax concession known as the Home Computer Initiative, whereby employers could provide computer equipment worth up to £2,500 to their staff. Employees could in effect buy computers at huge discounts to the shop price.

It was launched amid concerns about Britain's "digital divide" and was meant to encourage employees to become more IT literate. Unfortunately, the initiative was suddenly withdrawn in April 2006 on the grounds that it had already achieved its aim and had become poorly targeted.

However, that does not mean computers are no longer tax-free. If your employer provides you with a laptop or other such device to take home each evening or to work from home, it will not be a taxable benefit provided that:

- The computer was provided for work purposes, and
- Any private use is insignificant

The word "insignificant" is not defined in the legislation and is open to interpretation. In practice, it would depend on how much the computer is actually used for work purposes. If it is a necessary tool of the job, then it is likely that any domestic use would be seen as insignificant, should such a query arise in the first place.

To cover yourself in this situation, in particular if you're a home-worker, it is always best to sign a statement acknowledging receipt of the computer and confirming the following:

- The make/model and serial number of the computer
- A list of the main tasks for which it will be used
- The fact that it belongs to the employer
- That any private use must be insignificant
- That the computer will be returned on demand

This should deflect any suggestion by the taxman that home computers are taxable benefits.

Chapter 9

Work Canteens

Employers have always been allowed to run subsidised workplace canteens for their staff without a taxable benefit arising. This applies even if the meals are provided free of charge.

The main condition is that the facilities must be made available to **all** employees at that location and must not be reserved for a chosen few.

The meals do not have to be provided on the employer's premises but must be served in a staff canteen, not a public food outlet such as a restaurant, café or sandwich bar.

Employers are still allowed to segregate their staff without falling foul of the above condition.

For example, directors and senior management often eat in separate dining rooms with a dedicated table service.

However, the meals must not be on an unreasonable scale with elaborate menus and fine wines.

It is also permitted for employers to offer different levels of subsidy to their staff. For example, directors might eat free of charge whilst other staff have to make a small contribution.

Provided that free or subsidised meals are available to **all** staff the tax-free exemption will still apply.

Any payments made directly to an employee for the purpose of buying meals at work are not covered by this exemption. They should go through the payroll as with any other type of cash allowance and taxed as normal. The same goes for employer contributions to smart cards or other accounts used to buy meals.

It is no longer possible for employees to pay for meals at work through a salary sacrifice scheme. This was once a tax-efficient way of topping-up your lunch card for the staff canteen but has been banned since April 2011.

Chapter 10

Job-Related Accommodation

Living accommodation provided by your employer free of charge or at a below-market rent is *normally* treated as a taxable benefit. Indeed, there are special rules that dictate how this benefit is assessed. However, job-related accommodation is tax-free as long as it satisfies at least one of the following conditions:

- It is **necessary** for the proper performance of the employee's duties that he/she should reside in the accommodation, or

- The accommodation is provided for the **better performance** of the employee's duties and the employment is of a kind for which it is **customary** for accommodation to be provided, or

- There is a **special threat** to the employee's security and the accommodation is provided as part of security arrangements.

Where any of these conditions apply, any council tax or water rates relating to the property that are borne by the employer are also tax-free, as are expenses that would normally be the landlord's responsibility, such as external maintenance.

However, the employee would still be taxed on any other expenses paid for by the employer such as heating, lighting, cleaning, repairs (other than those listed above), decorating, furniture, kitchen equipment, or consumer durables such as televisions and computers, subject to a maximum limit of 10% of your net earnings (after deducting any personal contributions you make towards those costs).

The first two conditions listed above do not apply to directors unless they have no material interest in the company (i.e., do not own more than 5% of the shares) and are either full-time working directors or the company is non-profit or a charity.

Obviously it would be difficult for most jobs to meet those conditions and they really only apply to people such as school caretakers, gamekeepers or those serving in the armed forces.

Chapter 11

Business Trips and Holidays

This is a rather tricky area as holidays paid by your employer are most definitely taxable benefits whilst genuine business trips are not. However, it is sometimes possible to combine the two.

The key factor is the **main purpose** of the trip. If you go on a genuine business trip and take a few extra days holiday, or use the time between meetings to go sight-seeing, this will not be treated as a taxable benefit (but see below about expenses).

On the other hand, if you book a holiday and take the chance to visit a few people to discuss business, your employer cannot pay for the flight or hotel without a taxable benefit arising.

In between these two extremes lie many different situations where the main purpose of the trip is not clear-cut. In some cases the trip might be 50% business. You would probably get away with this provided you did not do it too often.

In the travel industry it is quite common for employers to send staff on "familiarisation trips". These are very popular and would be seen as a holiday in all but name by many people.

However, they can usually go down as genuine business trips, especially if organised by a third party, so long as there are no strong reasons for the taxman to suppose otherwise.

Employers should give staff planned itineraries before they go abroad for pre-arranged meetings, make sure they stay in contact with their colleagues by email while they are away to discuss business and ask them to file reports when they get back.

You should always pay any costs that are 100% for private leisure yourself, even if the trip itself is non-taxable. These would include internal flights, taxis, excursions and hotels for additional nights.

If the trip is mainly a holiday and is not tax-free, you can still claim expenses from your employer for additional costs such as travel to business meetings, hotel internet or client entertainment.

Chapter 12

Cheap Loans

Loans from your employer are normally a taxable benefit if you pay less than the "official" rate of interest on them (currently 4%). However, they are tax-free provided you owe your employer no more than £5,000 for the whole of the tax year.

This is still enough to cover most season ticket loans (just about) but the tax-free threshold is going up to £10,000 on 6 April 2014 after having been frozen at £5,000 since 1994/95.

Even if the loan is more than £5,000 you may still be able to avoid a taxable benefit if it's just a short-term loan. This is because the value of the benefit is assessed according to the number of **complete** months that the loan is outstanding, measured from the 6th of one month to the 5th of the next.

However, the taxman does have the option of substituting a more precise method based on the number of days the loan was actually outstanding, so any really large loans may still be taxable if they come to HMRC's attention.

It should be borne in mind that loans are aggregated for the purpose of deciding whether or not they exceed £5,000. Therefore, if you have a season ticket loan of £3,000 and a car loan of £3,000 you will be over the limit and both loans will be taxable benefits (unless of course you pay at least 4% interest on them).

Qualifying loans are always tax free. These are loans provided for business purposes, such as buying shares in a close company (small company), acquiring an interest in a partnership or providing funds to a business carried on in the UK by the borrower for trading purposes (where the interest is tax deductible).

Those working for banks and other financial institutions may be able to take advantage of another exemption if their loans are on similar terms to those made by their employer to the public at large in the ordinary course of business. This would be beneficial if the "official rate" happens to be higher than commercial rates of interest on such loans.

Chapter 13

Long-Service Awards

Anyone who has been employed by the same company (or companies in the same group) for 20 years or more is entitled to a tax-free long-service award. As well as regular employees, this applies to directors, even if they happen to own the company.

The exemption usually applies to gifts of tangible assets awarded as a testimonial to mark long service. It does not apply to cash payments or liabilities paid on your behalf, which are taxed in full.

Assets readily convertible into cash such as diamonds or precious metals do qualify for the exemption, but only up to the tax-free limit. Any excess would be taxed out of your normal earnings. The same applies to premium bonds, National Savings Certificates and shares or other securities in companies other than your employer.

The tax-free limit has been fixed at **£50 per year of service** since 2003, so if you have worked somewhere for 20 years you are entitled to a gift worth up to £1,000. Any excess would be taxed.

You would then qualify for another tax-free gift of £1,500 after a further 10 years of service, based on your total length of service at that stage (30 x £50). The tax-free amount is not reduced by the award you received after 20 years.

And if you work somewhere for 40 years you will qualify for another tax-free award worth £2,000 (40 x £50).

Thus you could potentially receive three tax-free awards worth a total of £4,500:

20 years – 20 x £50 = £1,000
30 years – 30 x £50 = £1,500
40 years – 40 x £50 = £2,000
Total   £4,500

Any subsequent awards received before 10 years have passed, for example after 25 years, would be taxed in full, regardless of whether the previous award used up the £50 per year tax-free limit or not.

They could also compromise the tax-free status of future awards, as there must be a 10-year gap between tax-free awards, even if the previous award was taxed in full. It's an all-or-nothing rule.

Long-service awards can also be given in the form of shares in the employing company (or another in the same group). However, the shares would be subject to capital gains tax when they are eventually sold, whereas most personal possessions are exempt (provided they are wasting assets or worth £6,000 or less).

Part-time workers are just as much entitled to this exemption as full-time staff. There is no minimum hours requirement.

Chapter 14

Staff Suggestion Schemes

Staff suggestion schemes tend to have a rather old-fashioned image these days, but the cardboard box in the staff canteen is pretty much a thing of the past. The concept has been revolutionised by modern communications.

There are two types of suggestion scheme award that are tax-free. The first is known as an **encouragement award** and is only worth £25. Any payments in excess of that would be taxed as earnings in the normal way. However, you can earn £25 as many times as you like without a tax charge arising.

The second type is known as a **financial benefit award** and is potentially worth much more. You can earn up to £5,000 tax-free with these.

Of course, there are conditions for both types of award. Firstly, the suggestion scheme must be open to all employees, either in the organisation as a whole or at a particular location.

Secondly, it must relate to activities carried on by your employer. Thirdly, the suggestion must be outside the scope of your normal duties. It must not be something that you are paid to do as part of your job. Lastly, the suggestion must not have been made at a meeting held for the purpose of proposing suggestions!

An encouragement award can be paid tax-free whether the suggestion is adopted or not. It is merely required to have special merit or be a "praiseworthy effort" by the person suggesting it.

A financial benefit award must be implemented by the employer and must be based on a likely degree of improvement in efficiency or effectiveness. This can be measured in terms of the prospective financial benefits or by the importance of the subject matter.

The award cannot exceed 50% of the net financial benefit during the first year of implementation or 10% over a period of up to five years, subject to the maximum tax-free payment of £5,000.

Chapter 15

Gyms & Sports Facilities

Many large companies have on-site gyms or run sporting facilities on behalf of their staff such as playing fields, clubhouses and squash courts. These are tax-free provided that they are:

- Generally available to **all** employees
- Not provided on domestic premises
- Not generally available to the public at large
- Not used for holidays or overnight accommodation
- Not vehicles or vessels such as go-karts or motor boats

In practice, this means that sports facilities must be on premises owned or rented by the employer or by a few employers clubbing together.

Unfortunately, membership of local sports or fitness clubs is not usually tax-free as they are open to the public too.

However, such memberships may be tax-free if employees are only allowed to use the facilities at particular times when they are closed to the general public.

It is also necessary for the membership contract to be in the employer's name, not those of its employees.

It is permitted for non-employees to use the facilities provided that they are local residents and public access is restricted to them and/or certain other identifiable groups. This is a useful measure that can allow external funding of the facilities.

Personal trainers, tennis coaches, etc are also covered by the exemption provided that they are hired by the employer and the cost does not include subscriptions or entry fees for premises open to the general public at the same time.

Leisure facilities such as bars, lounges, pool tables and TV sports channels are covered by the exemption subject to the same rules as above. Furthermore, food and drink consumed on these premises is tax free if it is available to all employees generally.

Chapter 16

Relocation Expenses

As one might expect, expenses incurred by your employer (or reimbursed to you) when you move to a different location due to the demands of your job are generally tax-free.

However, many people would be surprised to know that there is a limit on this, and it has been pegged at **£8,000** since 1993.

Obviously the move has to be caused by your job, not vice versa. You cannot decide to move to another part of the country, find a new job and then claim tax-free removal expenses, even if you found an employer generous enough to pay them.

You would have to move home in order to:

- Take up a new job with a new employer,

- Take up a new job with your existing employer, or

- Continue with your current job but at a new location

Your existing home must not be within reasonable daily travelling distance of your new workplace, whilst your new home obviously must, otherwise the relocation would not be caused by your job.

What counts as reasonable travelling distance is not defined, but each case would be decided on its own merits.

You must also treat the new home as your main residence. If you only stay there during the week and then return to your existing home at weekends, with no intention of moving permanently, the exemption will not apply.

There is no requirement to actually sell your existing home, however. You can keep it if you wish.

It is worth noting that your employer must actually reimburse you for relocation expenses. You cannot bear the cost yourself and then claim them against tax on your earnings.

Most expenses relating to the disposal of your existing home and acquisition of a new one are covered by the exemption, including:

1. Legal fees
2. Selling costs
3. Stamp duty land tax
4. Bridging loan finance
5. Hotels
6. Travel
7. Removal/storage costs, and
8. Replacement of domestic goods that cannot easily be moved such as carpets, curtains and cookers

Unless there are exceptional circumstances, all removal costs must be incurred by the end of the tax year following the one in which you started your new job (or changed your workplace).

Therefore, you have between one and two years to receive relocation benefits tax free.

Chapter 17

Eye Tests & Health Care

Although health insurance and medical care are taxable benefits, there are a few health-related benefits (e.g. annual flu jabs) that are tax free.

These are all costs that are relevant to your employment and are therefore seen as legitimate business expenses.

Eye tests are the most relevant cost for most people. Your employer can reimburse the cost of an eye test without a taxable benefit arising, if it is required by health and safety legislation.

This would apply to anyone using display screen equipment.

The same goes for corrective appliances that are solely required for the purposes of your job, for example if they were necessary to do VDU work.

Your employer may pay for them on a tax-free basis and any vouchers that they give you to buy them are also tax free.

However, in most cases, spectacles or contact lenses are prescribed for general use too, and these are not tax-free benefits.

The only exception is if they include a **special** prescription for VDU use, in which case the relevant proportion of the cost will be tax free.

Your employer can also pay for a) medicals and b) health screening assessments without a taxable benefit arising.

However, you can only have **one** of each type during the tax year on a tax-free basis.

There is no requirement to undergo a health screening assessment first in order for a medical check-up to qualify for the exemption.

In addition, medical treatment whilst you are working abroad can be paid by your employer tax free provided that:

- Your absence is due to the requirements of your job, and

- The need for the treatment **first** arises while you are outside the UK by reason of your employment.

The exemption also applies to the cost of providing insurance against the cost of such treatment whilst you are working abroad.

Finally, you can claim for the cost of any inoculations or drugs (such as malaria tablets) recommended for the part of the world you are travelling to by reason of your employment without a taxable benefit arising.

However, the **main** purpose of your trip must be for business. You cannot claim this for holidays.

Chapter 18

Staff Parties

Your employer can pay for a Christmas party or a "similar annual function" such as a summer barbecue on a tax-free basis, provided that the cost per head does not exceed **£150**. This has been the limit since April 2003 and is still enough for most employers.

The key word here is **annual**. The exemption does not apply to non-annual events such as staff parties to mark the 5th anniversary of a business or to irregular events such as staff leaving drinks.

On the other hand, it does not need to be a party as such. A similar annual function could be a staff day out or a visit to the theatre.

The event must be open to **all** employees generally or to those at a particular location. Where employees belong to particular sections or departments, you can have a separate party for each one so long as everyone is invited to at least one.

You are not restricted to just one event a year. The exemption can be split across more than one event during the tax year provided that they are all annual. Of course, the more events you have the more difficult it may be to prove that they all qualify.

The £150 is all-inclusive and covers extras such as raffle prizes, gifts, taxi fares and overnight accommodation. Small gifts/prizes may be tax-free anyway as "trivial expenses".

The total cost of the event includes VAT so this must be added back to the net cost if it is recoverable by the employer.

The total cost must be divided by the number of persons present to determine the cost per head. Note that this does not have to be just employees. It can also include guests such as husbands, wives, and other partners, so in this respect, the more the merrier.

In fact, customers, suppliers and other non-employees can also be invited provided it fundamentally remains a staff event. This may help to keep the cost per head below the £150 tax-free limit.

A word of warning, though. If the cost per head exceeds £150 the whole lot becomes a taxable benefit, not just the excess.

If that looks like happening, it may be wise for employers to levy a small personal contribution on each attendee in advance. Alternatively, they could insist that taxis and hotels are paid for by the guests to keep the overall cost down.

In practice, employers often pay the tax on staff entertainment or annual events above the £150 exemption on behalf of their staff by special arrangement with HMRC. It is highly unlikely that you would find yourself paying extra tax simply because of the generosity of your employer.

This is for practical reasons more than anything else, as it is very difficult to apportion the cost of an event between employees on a fair and equitable basis.

Chapter 19

Bicycles

An employer may lend or hire bicycles (plus safety equipment) to employees without any taxable benefit arising, provided that:

- They are available to all employees generally, and

- The employee uses the bicycle mainly for qualifying journeys

Qualifying journeys mean travelling between home and work or between different workplaces. They also include travel between the workplace and local amenities (no more than 10 miles away) such as shops and leisure centres during working hours.

It is not necessary to keep a record of qualifying journeys just to prove that the main use test is satisfied. In practice, the taxman will not challenge any scheme where an employer makes bicycles available to its staff unless there is very strong evidence to show that they are used mainly for non-qualifying journeys.

You will not lose the exemption just because you use the bike for other purposes too, or lend it to your friends or family. However, you may lose the exemption if you work at home most of the time, or if you regularly use the bike to take part in organised cycling events.

It should be noted that the exemption does not apply to bicycles that are **given** to the employee rather than hired or lent. This would be a taxable benefit just like any other asset made available to an employee for their private use.

The bicycles do not need to be offered to employees on exactly the same terms and conditions. For example, employees participating in a salary sacrifice arrangement may be offered better bicycles than those who are not.

However, employees unable to participate (such as those aged under 18 without an adult guarantor) must still have access to a bicycle from their employer if they wish to use one.

Also, a bicycle does not have to be offered to each employee for their **sole** use. An employer could simply have a pool of bicycles that are available to all employees at a particular location.

Sadly, the concession allowing tax free breakfasts on designated "Cycle to Work" days was scrapped with effect from 6th April 2012.

Chapter 20

Public Transport

Generally, you are taxed on any travel costs borne by your employer for "ordinary commuting" between home and work, as such costs are not deductible against your earnings.

However, there are certain circumstances where this rule does not apply.

Travel between home and a **temporary** workplace is not classified by the taxman as "ordinary commuting". Therefore, any travel and subsistence costs paid or reimbursed by your employer are tax-free. The rules for this are very complex, however.

Works buses are tax-free so long as they are made available to all employees generally for "qualifying journeys". Basically, this means travel between home and a workplace, including journeys that are completed only partly by the bus.

The service must be used **mainly** for "qualifying journeys" by employees and their children. Occasional use by non-employees will not result in the exemption being lost. Neither will non-qualifying journeys, so long as the main use test is met.

It is the bus service that is exempt, not the bus itself, so any other use is taxable. The vehicle used to provide the service must be a bus with seats for 12 passengers or a minibus with seats for nine (plus the driver).

Your employer can also reimburse you for additional costs without a taxable benefit arising if public transport is disrupted by strikes or other industrial action. This can include taxis, hotels or other overnight accommodation at or near your place of work.

Offshore oil and gas workers enjoy a special exemption from the ordinary commuting rule as any transport provided by the employer between the mainland and the rig is a tax-free benefit.

There are also special rules for those on overseas assignments (see Chapter 32).

Late-night taxis remain tax-free provided you satisfy the strict conditions. The main ones are that you are required to work later than 9pm on an **irregular** basis and that it would not be reasonable for you to use trains or buses at that time of night.

There were plans to abolish this exemption but the Government had to backtrack as it would have compromised the safety of "vulnerable groups". But the rules on late-night taxis have been tightened up a lot in recent years anyway. You can no longer assume that up to 60 taxis a year are tax-free as you could before.

Chapter 21

Counselling

Many large employers offer their staff counselling services on a range of issues, usually by way of telephone help-lines followed by face-to-face meetings with specialist advisers. These are commonly known as Employee Assistance Programmes.

These programmes typically deal with issues such as stress at work, debt problems, drug or alcohol dependency, ill-health, bullying, sexual harassment, bereavement, disciplinary matters, career concerns, equal opportunities and personal relationships.

Advice on these and similar issues provided by the employer will not give rise to a taxable benefit so long as it does not include advice on financial planning, tax/legal affairs, leisure/recreation activities or medical treatment of any kind.

A good example I came across a few years ago was an employee who was afraid of flying. For many years this only caused him a problem with holidays, but then it became necessary for him to attend regular meetings in Shannon, on the west coast of Ireland.

The only way he could get there was to drive to Wales, take the ferry, drive across Ireland, and then repeat the journey back home again. Clearly this caused a major problem at work, not least because he needed to take a whole day off just to get there.

His boss sent him to a psychiatrist who managed to convince him that his fear of flying could be controlled. Soon he was booking flights with no anxiety whatsoever. Clearly that was a tax-free counselling service even though flying is usually recreational.

However, the dividing line between exempt and non-exempt counselling is not always so clear-cut. Sometimes, employees may have domestic problems that are not covered by the exemption but which then spill over into problems at work, or vice-versa.

In such circumstances, the work problems cannot be dealt with separately by the Employee Assistance Programme as they are linked inextricably to the other issues.

For example, drug addiction may cause an employee to run up mortgage debts and eventually face eviction from his home. It may be necessary to give him legal advice to deal with the immediate problem, even though the underlying cause was drug addiction.

In those circumstances, it may be difficult to distinguish how and when the advice changes from drug dependency to legal matters, especially if both issues are covered in the same meeting.

HMRC has therefore agreed guidelines with the UK Employee Assistance Professionals Association to cover such situations. It has been specifically agreed that legal information provided within the context of welfare counselling for employees is exempt so long as it remains within clear guidelines.

These guidelines can be found on the following HMRC webpage:

www.hmrc.gov.uk/specialist/welfare-counselling.pdf

Generally, the legal advice must be related to an emotional issue rather than a commercial one and provided within the framework of a 'signposting' service. In other words, the counsellor should refer the caller to an information specialist who will be able to give them the detailed advice they need.

There are also strict rules on the extent to which counselling services can be given to an employee's immediate family, even though they may be responsible for the emotional issues affecting the employee's performance at work.

Chapter 22

Redundancy Training

"Outplacement" training is often offered to employees who are made redundant or lose their jobs for some other reason. The courses are normally run by specialist agencies with the aim of helping employees a) adjust to the termination of their employment, b) pick up new skills and c) find new jobs.

Generally these services are tax-free if paid for directly by the employer. However, there are some conditions that must be met:

- The only or main purpose of providing these services must be to enable the employee to adjust to losing their job and/or find a new job (or to become self-employed),

- The services must consist wholly of a) giving guidance and advice, b) imparting or improving skills or c) providing or making available computers or similar facilities,

- The person receiving the services must have been an employee throughout the **2 years** ending either a) when the services begin or b) when the employment terminated (if earlier), and

- The services must be generally available to all employees or a particular class of employee.

It is important to remember that it must be the employer who pays for the outplacement services. Tax relief is not available if the employee is simply given a cash allowance out of which to pay for such services, or indeed pays for them personally without any assistance from the employer at all.

However, even if the employer does not offer to pay for the services, it may still agree to pay for them and deduct the cost from any monies owed to you, such as redundancy pay.

The advantage of this is that they may well be able to reclaim the VAT charged by the service provider and only deduct the net amount, whereas you would be unable to reclaim VAT at all.

Chapter 23

Life Insurance

Many large employers provide staff with group life cover that pays out to families in the event of death or terminal illness. Usually this benefit is part of their standard employment contract.

These schemes can be worth a lot of money over a period of 25 to 30 years as the employee is spared the cost of having to arrange their own cover.

The benefit is tax free under current legislation, as are any benefits paid out. There is no need to report them on P11Ds or declare them on your tax return.

Until recently, small companies were unable to take advantage of these schemes as they were only open to large employers. However, many life companies have now developed products known as Relevant Life Plans which are specifically designed for small companies. Provided certain legal conditions are met, the plans enjoy the same tax advantages as the larger schemes.

The following illustration is taken from a 2012 Legal & General booklet explaining the benefits of their Relevant Life Plan.

	Typical Life Policy	Relevant Life Plan
Annual premium	£1,000	£1,000
Employee NI (2%)	£34.48	None
Income tax (40%)	£689.65	None
Required earnings	£1,724.13	£1,000
Employer NI (13.8%)	£237.93	None
Total gross cost	£1,962.06	£1,000
Corporation tax relief	£392.41	£200
Total cost	**£1,569.65**	**£800**

As you can see, the Relevant Life Plan is almost 50% cheaper than a policy not qualifying for the advantageous tax treatment.

Chapter 24

Gifts & Entertainment

Many people ask what the tax position is if they receive gifts or entertainment from their employer, customers or suppliers. It depends on a) their value and nature, b) who is providing them, and c) the circumstances in which they are given.

Anything received from your employer is normally taxable as part of your earnings if it was by reason of your employment (which goes without saying in most cases as you would not be getting it in the first place if you were not an employee).

The good news is that entertainment provided by your employer is normally tax-free for you personally as it is either covered by the *annual functions* exemption (see Chapter 18) or any tax liability is paid by your employer under a PAYE Settlement Agreement.

This is a special arrangement between your employer and HM Revenue & Customs to pay any tax that may arise on certain benefits-in-kind on behalf of their employees.

Likewise, small gifts are usually exempt as *trivial benefits* (see Chapter 25). For example, flowers sent to an employee who has suffered a bereavement, or bottles of wine given away to staff at Christmas, will count as trivial benefits.

However, if you regularly enjoy lavish entertainment courtesy of your employer or receive expensive gifts, it would be wise to check the tax position. In many cases, particularly with small employers, they may not even know the tax rules themselves!

Generally though, you will only be taxed on benefits reported on your annual P11D. The onus is on your employer to get this right, not you, so any such items not reported when they should have been will be their responsibility, not yours.

In those circumstances, your employer would have to pay tax and national insurance on the "grossed-up" value of the benefit, not the actual value you received.

Entertainment provided by third parties (such as customers or suppliers) is normally tax-free, subject to the following:

- The third party is not **connected** with your employer (or employs your employer),

- Your employer has not **procured** the entertainment on behalf of the third party, either directly or indirectly, and

- The entertainment is not provided in payment or recognition of any particular services that you have performed (or will perform) in the course of your employment.

Gifts from third parties are also tax-free subject to the above. In addition, however, the gifts must not be in cash (or vouchers that can be exchanged for cash) and must not exceed **£250** per annum.

Chapter 25

Trivial Benefits

Anything that can be classified as a trivial benefit is exempt from tax and should not appear on your P11D. This sensible measure avoids items such as leaving gifts, flowers, office refreshments or the occasional working lunch from being taxable benefits.

The HMRC guidance is a bit sketchy on this subject and only gives common examples, such as small Christmas gifts, tea and coffee, water, flu jabs and flowers. Other items qualify as well though.

HMRC specifically states that there are instances where employers have to apply common sense and judgement. In particular, there is no set monetary limit. This is probably just as well, because if there was it would no doubt have been frozen for many years now!

It is the cost per head that decides whether a benefit is trivial or not. For example, a large employer may spend a lot providing each of its employees with a turkey at Christmas, but the value to each individual employee would be low.

Frequency is also a relevant factor. If small gifts are given out to employees several times a year for whatever reason, this may well tip the balance against them being trivial benefits.

Leaving gifts can be a grey area. Usually these are exempt, but large gifts may well be taxable. For example, a client of ours once gave a £400 SLR camera to an employee as a leaving gift. This was not exactly trivial by any stretch of the imagination.

Cash or shopping vouchers are **never** exempt as trivial benefits. Cash (or vouchers that can be converted to cash) should always go through the payroll, whilst shopping vouchers should always be treated as taxable benefits, no matter how low in value they are.

Likewise, anything that is specifically a reward to an employee for services performed should always be taxed as part of earnings. It can never be exempt as a trivial benefit. That would obviously cover prizes for work achievements such as meeting monthly sales targets, even if it is a very cheap item.

Part 3

Salary Sacrifice Schemes

Chapter 26

How Salary Sacrifice Works

Salary sacrifice schemes have become extremely common over the last 10 years and most large employers now offer them to their staff in some shape or form. As well as being tax efficient, they are also quite flexible and can be tailored to an employee's needs.

Salary sacrifice is a very effective way of boosting your disposable income when you take account of the cash that you would have spent on the benefit that is provided by your employer. But how do these schemes actually work?

Basically, what they do is substitute a benefit-in-kind for a given amount of salary. The tax saving comes about because the benefit you are gaining is either tax free or subject to a lower rate of tax and/or national insurance than the income you are giving up.

Your take home pay may well go down, but once you factor in the cash saving you make from no longer having to pay for that benefit yourself, your disposable income will increase.

If your income is between £50,000 and £60,000 a salary sacrifice scheme may also help you avoid the new child benefit tax charge.

The taxman gives his blessing to salary sacrifice schemes provided that the rules are strictly followed. There are **two** main conditions that must be observed.

Firstly, the benefit must qualify for favourable tax treatment, which normally means following all the conditions. For example, pension contributions must not exceed the annual allowance or lifetime allowance, and must be paid into an approved plan.

Secondly, your employment contract needs to be officially varied. This is normally achieved by both the employer and the employee signing a contract amendment before the scheme takes effect.

We will now look at how salary sacrifice schemes work with the three most popular types of benefit: pension contributions, childcare vouchers and company cars.

Chapter 27

Salary Sacrifice Pensions

These are far and away the most lucrative type of benefit for salary sacrifice schemes, due mainly to the fact that your employer can contribute up to £50,000 a year (£40,000 from 2014/15).

As most people are aware, all pension contributions offer income tax relief. But when your employer pays them on your behalf, there are also substantial **national insurance** savings to be had. It is these national insurance savings that make salary sacrifice pensions more attractive than making pension contributions yourself.

It is important to remember here that your employer also pays national insurance on your salary – at a rate of 13.8%. If you reduce your salary in return for pension contributions, your employer will pay less national insurance and can plough the savings back into your pension pot.

Of course, not all employers will choose to do this. Some may wish to keep the saving for themselves, but clearly there is scope for employers to pay more than the amount of salary sacrificed.

Basic-rate taxpayers tend to do quite well out of salary sacrifice schemes because their national insurance contributions are 12%, whereas higher-rate taxpayers only pay 2% national insurance on earnings over £41,450 (2013/14 figures).

On the debit side, however, you will lose the 25% top-up that the Government adds to your pension contributions if paid into a personal plan. Contributions by employers do not get this top-up. You will also lose any tax rebate you get for higher-rate relief.

You basically have three options:

- Keep your net pay at exactly the same level as it was before,

- Increase your net pay in return for lower contributions, or

- Reduce your net pay in return for higher contributions

The advantages of a salary sacrifice scheme are increased by maximising contributions. However, the following two examples will assume that the employee's net pay is the same both before and after the salary sacrifice.

Example 1 – Basic-Rate Taxpayer

Peter earns £25,000 per annum and pays £5,000 into a personal pension. His net pay after tax and national insurance is £19,819. His disposable income is therefore £14,819. The taxman adds basic-rate tax relief of £1,250 to his pension plan so the total sum invested is £6,250.

His employer sets up a salary sacrifice scheme and offers to add all his national insurance savings to Peter's pension. Peter joins the scheme but wishes to keep the same disposable income as before. To achieve this, his salary is reduced by £7,353 to £17,647. His employer saves national insurance of £1,015 (£7,353 x 13.8%) and the total pension contribution is £8,368 (£7,353 + £1,015).

The position before and after the salary sacrifice is shown in the table below:

	Before £	After £
Salary	25,000	17,647
Income tax	-3,112	-1,641
Employee NI	-2,069	-1,187
Net pay	19,819	14,819
Pension contribution	-5,000	0
Disposable income	14,819	14,819
Employee contribution	5,000	0
HMRC top-up	1,250	0
Employer contribution	0	7,353
Employer NI saving	0	1,015
Total investment	6,250	8,368

Peter's disposable income is exactly the same as before, but his pension fund has increased by £2,118 – an increase of 34%.

Over 10 years, assuming annual growth in the pension fund of 5%, this would produce an extra £26,800.

Example 2 – Higher-Rate Taxpayer

Paul earns £55,000 per annum and pays £5,000 into a personal pension. His net pay after tax and national insurance is £38,864.

His pension contribution is grossed up by £1,250 so the total sum invested is £6,250. However, being a higher-rate taxpayer, he also gets a rebate from the taxman of £1,250. His disposable income is therefore £38,864 - £5,000 + £1,250 = £35,114.

His employer sets up a salary sacrifice scheme and offers to contribute all the national insurance savings to Paul's pension.

Paul joins the scheme but wishes to keep the same disposable income as before. To achieve this, his salary is reduced by £6,465 to £48,535. At 13.8% the national insurance saving is £892 and the total pension contribution is £7,357.

The position before and after the salary sacrifice is shown in the table below:

	Before	**After**
	£	£
Salary	55,000	48,535
Income tax	-11,822	-9,236
Employee NI	-4,314	-4,185
Net pay	38,864	35,114
Pension contribution	-5,000	0
Tax rebate	1,250	0
Disposable income	35,114	35,114
Employee contribution	5,000	0
HMRC top-up	1,250	0
Employer contribution	0	6,465
Employer NI saving	0	892
Total investment	6,250	7,357

Paul's disposable income is exactly the same as before, but his pension fund has increased by £1,107 – an increase of nearly 18%.

Clearly basic-rate taxpayers do much better than higher-rate taxpayers from employer pension contributions funded by salary sacrifice.

Higher-rate taxpayers personally save only 2% national insurance, not 12% – most of the benefit only arises if your employer agrees to pay his 13.8% national insurance saving into your pension pot.

As already mentioned, not all employers are willing to do this, not the whole 13.8% at any rate. Therefore, the savings could be much lower, especially for higher-rate taxpayers.

Nevertheless, if your employer does agree to pass on the whole of his national insurance saving, an 18% increase in your pension pot is an extremely good result.

Compulsory Pensions

Compulsory pension contributions (known as auto-enrolment) are being phased in between October 2012 and April 2017. Employers will have to start off paying 1%, rising to 3% from October 2018, and employees will have to contribute a similar amount.

You should therefore be careful about locking into a salary sacrifice arrangement for something that in due course you may get for free anyway. However, many salary sacrifice schemes only last for 12 months, after which you can opt out, so it may be worth it for a short time until your employer is auto-enrolled.

Also, it would still be worthwhile entering into a salary sacrifice scheme, even after auto-enrolment, if you wish to contribute more than the prescribed percentage of salary to your pension scheme.

Alternatively, you could just opt out of auto-enrolment and rely instead on a salary sacrifice scheme. However, you would then lose the benefit of the free employer contributions.

For more information, see the Taxcafe guide *Pension Magic*.

Chapter 28

Childcare Vouchers

This is probably the next most popular benefit offered by salary sacrifice schemes – not surprisingly, given the high cost of childcare these days and the fact that most people are parents at some stage in their lives.

As childcare costs are not tax deductible if you pay them yourself, you can save tax as well as national insurance by joining a salary sacrifice scheme.

The basic idea is the employee sacrifices some salary and in return the employer gives the employee a childcare voucher. The employee gives the voucher to a childcare provider. The childcare provider then sends the voucher with a bill to the employer to receive payment or redeems it with the vouchers company.

Tax-free Limits

Sadly, the tax free limit has been frozen at £55 per week (or £243 per month) since 2005. For higher-rate taxpayers not already in a scheme by 5th April 2011, the weekly limit is only £28 (or £124 per month) – and those lucky people paying 45% tax are only entitled to £25 per week (or £110 per month)!

Nonetheless, a basic-rate taxpayer could still save £933 a year in income tax and national insurance with a salary sacrifice scheme (£243 x 12 x 32%). If both parents receive childcare vouchers this saving doubles to £1,866.

A higher-rate taxpayer could save £625 a year in income tax and national insurance with a salary sacrifice scheme (£124 x 12 x 42%). If both parents receive childcare vouchers and they both pay higher-rate tax this saving doubles to £1,250.

An additional rate taxpayer saves £620 a year in income tax and national insurance with a salary sacrifice scheme (£110 x 12 x 47%) or £1,240 a year if both parents get them and pay 45% tax.

Effect on Tax Credits

Unfortunately, childcare vouchers can reduce your tax credits entitlement.

The childcare element of working tax credit offers up to 70% towards childcare costs. However, you can only claim the childcare element if you pay for childcare yourself. Childcare vouchers do not count.

On the other hand, because your salary is smaller under a salary sacrifice scheme, it is possible that your tax credits claim could actually *increase*. The vouchers do not count as earnings for the purpose of calculating your entitlement.

The big winners in this complex game of swings and roundabouts will be those people who:

- Previously had no childcare at all, or
- Use the vouchers to buy extra childcare, or
- Were not entitled to tax credits in the first place

The losers will be those who don't earn enough to pay tax or national insurance.

Example 1 - Low Income (with low childcare costs)

Jill is a single mother bringing up two children on her own. She works 35 hours per week and earns £8 per hour. For three days a week she receives free childcare at a state nursery. For the other two working days she pays a registered childminder £112 per week.

Her employer offers childcare vouchers worth £55 per week in exchange for an equivalent reduction in her wages. Should she accept them?

Step 1
Jill needs to work out her entitlement to tax credits before any reduction for being over the income limit. The total for a lone parent with 2 children working over 30 hours a week is **£10,665**.

Step 2
Then she must add on the childcare element. She pays £5,264 per annum to her childminder (she only needs her for 47 weeks during the year) and can recover 70%, which is **£3,685**.

Step 3
Now she needs to know how much to deduct. Her wages are £14,560 per annum and the income limit for working tax credit is £6,420. The difference of £8,140 is clawed back at 41% so **£3,337** is deducted from her entitlement.

Step 4
That gives her a total tax credits entitlement of **£11,013** per annum (being £10,665 plus £3,685 minus £3,337).

Step 5
Now she needs to work out her net pay for the year. Tax on her wages is £1,024 and national insurance is £817 (based on 2013/14 rates and allowances) so her net pay is **£12,719**.

Step 6
Her net income for the year is therefore **£23,732** (Step 4 + Step 5). Note that child benefit does not affect tax credits so is ignored.

Step 7
After paying the childminder, she is left with **£18,468** (being £23,732 minus the £5,264 from Step 2).

Step 8
If Jill accepts the childcare vouchers, her wages will drop to **£11,700** per annum. Note that this reduces her hourly rate to £6.43 as her total hours (including holidays) are 35 x 52 = 1,820.

Step 9
Her employer must check that her new hourly rate is not below the National Minimum Wage. The NMW rate for adults is currently £6.19 per hour, so at £6.43 she is still earning more than the minimum.

Step 10
Tax on her wages would be £452 and national insurance would be £474, giving her net pay of **£10,774** per annum.

Step 11
Her tax credits will go up as she now has a lower income. The increase will be **£1,173** (being £55 x 52 weeks = £2,860 x 41%), but note the new *disregard* rule for income reductions of up to £2,500 from 6th April 2012 onwards.

Step 12
The childcare element of her tax credits would decrease by **£2,002** per annum (being £55 x 52 weeks = £2,860 x 70%). This will kick in straight away and so affect the current year of her claim. Only changes in costs of £10 per week or less are ignored.

Step 13
Her tax credits next year will therefore drop to **£10,184** (being £11,013 from Step 4 plus £1,173 from Step 11 less £2,002 from Step 12).

Step 14
Jill's net annual income would now be only **£20,958** (being the net pay of £10,774 from Step 10 plus the £10,184 from Step 13).

Step 15
Her childcare costs will go down to **£2,404** (being the original cost of £5,264 from Step 2 less £55 x 52 weeks for the vouchers).

Step 16
After paying the childminder £2,404, she is left with **£18,554** (compared with the £18,468 from Step 7).

Conclusion: Jill is £86 a year better off with the vouchers based on 2013/14 rates/allowances.

Example 2
Average Income (with high childcare costs)

Jim and Jane have three children of whom one is below school age. They both work full-time and their joint income is £40,000 per annum. They pay a nursery an average £200 a week for the youngest child.

Their employer offers them each childcare vouchers worth £55 a week in exchange for an equivalent reduction in their salaries. Should they accept the vouchers?

Step 1
First they must calculate their entitlement to tax credits before any reduction for being over the income limit. The total for a couple with three children working over 30 hours a week is **£13,385**.

Step 2
Then they must add on the childcare element. The maximum eligible cost for one child is £175 per week which is £9,100 a year. They can recover 70% of this, which is **£6,370**.

Step 3
Now they need to know how much to deduct. Their joint income is £40,000 per annum and the income limit for working tax credit is £6,420. The difference of £33,580 is clawed back at 41% so **£13,767** is deducted from their entitlement.

Step 4
That gives Jim and Jane a total tax credits entitlement of **£5,988** per annum (being £13,385 + £6,370 - £13,767).

Step 5
Now they need to work out their net pay for the year. Tax on their salaries is £4,224 and national insurance is £2,939 (based on 2013/14 rates and allowances) so their net pay is **£32,837**.

Step 6
Their net annual income is therefore **£38,825** (Step 4 + Step 5). Note that child benefit does not affect tax credits so is ignored.

Step 7
After paying the nursery £10,400 (£200 x 52 weeks) they are left with **£28,425**.

Step 8
If Jim and Jane accept the childcare vouchers, their joint income (for tax credit purposes) will go down by £5,720 (being £55 x 2 x 52 weeks) to £34,280. This will increase their tax credits by **£2,345** (being £5,720 x 41%), as long as they avoid the disregard rule.

Step 9
Their childcare costs would drop to **£4,680** per annum (being the £10,400 from Step 7 minus £55 x 52 weeks x 2 for the vouchers).

Step 10
The childcare element of their tax credits would be only £3,276 (being the £4,680 from Step 9 x 70%). This is a reduction of **£3,094**.

Step 11
Their total tax credits would therefore be **£5,239** (being the £5,988 from Step 4 plus £2,345 from Step 8 less £3,094 from Step 10).

Step 12
They would pay tax of £3,080 and national insurance of £2,253 on their salaries – so their total net pay would be **£28,947**.

Step 13
Their total income would therefore be **£34,186** (being the £5,239 from Step 11 plus the £28,947 from Step 12).

Step 14
After paying the nursery £4,680 as calculated in Step 9, this leaves them with **£29,506** (compared to the £28,425 from Step 7).

Conclusion: Jim and Jane are £1,081 a year better off with the vouchers based on 2013/14 rates/allowances.

Why Do Jim and Jane Do Better?

The reason why Jim and Jane do so much better with vouchers than Jill is because they are already paying more than the maximum eligible cost for childcare (£200 per week compared with the maximum eligible cost of £175 per week).

Therefore by taking childcare vouchers they do not lose 70% of the extra £25 they pay because they were never receiving tax credits for that extra cost in the first place.

Analysis of the Examples

It may seem surprising that in both of the examples above it was better to take childcare vouchers, given the widely different circumstances. In both cases, the extra income came about as follows:

- Tax and national insurance saving on the salary sacrifice
- *Plus* reduced income restriction due to a lower salary
- *Less* reduced childcare element due to the vouchers

This calculation is summarised in the table below.

	Example 1	**Example 2**	**Per £100**
Reduced tax and NI	+£915	+£1,830	+£32
Income restriction	+£1,173	+£2,345	+£41
Childcare element	-£2,002	-£3,094	-£70
Additional income	+£86	+£1,081	+£3

If Jim and Jane had not already been paying more than the maximum for one child of £175, the reduction in their childcare element would have been £4,004 and their additional income would have been only £171 (i.e. twice that of Jill).

It should be noted that the above table only applies if you satisfy **all** of the following criteria:

- You are a basic-rate taxpayer
- You sacrifice the same amount of salary
- Your annual income is higher than £9,280
- You are not affected by the income disregard rule

Annual income for this purpose is that relevant for tax credits. For example, it does not include child benefit or bank interest of less than £300 a year.

From the last column, you will see that most people are better off with childcare vouchers by £3 for each £100 of vouchers given.

The +£32 represents 20% tax plus 12% national insurance. The +£41 is the 41% income restriction and the -£70 is the 70% lost on the childcare costs.

Effect on Low Earners

Some low earners may lose out with childcare vouchers for the following reasons:

- They do not pay much tax and national insurance on their earnings anyway (so there is less to save), and

- Their tax credits are less affected by the income restriction of £6,420 (so again there is less to save)

However, if they take childcare vouchers the 70% support for childcare costs would still be reduced. It would be all swings and no roundabouts!

The Disregard Rule

Tax credit claims are initially based on your income from the *previous tax year*. If your income falls this year (for example, because you join a salary sacrifice scheme) you may have to wait until next year before you see an increase in your tax credits.

It is only if your income falls significantly (by more than £2,500) that your tax credit entitlement for the current year is determined by your income for the current year. The first £2,500 of any fall in income is, however, disregarded.

This is very important when it comes to timing your decision to accept childcare vouchers.

Look again at the above table showing the effect of childcare vouchers on household income. The +£41 for the income restriction would disappear for the first year, leaving you not £3 better off for each £100 worth of vouchers but £38 worse off!

At £3 per year for each £100, it would take you another 13 years to recover that loss, assuming the rules aren't changed again.

Incidentally, the disregard rule does not apply to your childcare costs. The reduction in the childcare element kicks in straight away. You will therefore lose 70% of the value of the vouchers immediately with no compensating adjustment to your tax credits.

The only way to avoid that is to spend the vouchers on *additional childcare*, thus not saving anything, or if your existing childcare costs are so far above the maximum eligible amounts that the vouchers make no difference.

You can avoid the negative effect of the disregard rule on childcare vouchers in a salary sacrifice scheme in the following situations:

- Your actual income for the year goes up (or would have gone up) by at least the amount of the vouchers.

- Your income would have gone down by at least £2,500 anyway even without the reduction from a salary sacrifice scheme.

The first situation would apply if, for example, you are offered a choice between a pay rise or childcare vouchers. However, you should bear in mind that there is also a disregard rule for *increases* in relevant income of up to £10,000. This means your tax credits would not have been affected by the pay rise anyway, at least not for the current year.

You might think that if you can get childcare vouchers in exchange for a pay rise and there is no change to your tax credits (ignoring the childcare element) then that is a good result. In the long run it would be, but for the current year you would actually be worse off, as any saving in tax and national insurance would be more than offset by the reduction in the childcare element.

Employer Contributions

So far we have assumed that in a salary sacrifice scheme you would give up an equivalent amount of salary for childcare vouchers, but you may do even better. Your employer will also save 13.8% national insurance and may choose to pass on some of this saving to you by making the salary sacrifice smaller.

Summary

If you are offered childcare vouchers in a salary sacrifice scheme and it affects your tax credits, it is normally only worthwhile accepting them if:

- You do so **before** renewing your tax credits application for the current year, **and**

- You renew them based on your **expected** income for the **current** year rather than based on your known income for the previous year.

Otherwise, you will probably be caught by the new disregard rule for income reductions of up to £2,500. The only way you can really avoid this is if you reduce your income just *before* the end of the current year of claim, so the effect is minimised.

It is also worth bearing in mind that childcare vouchers are **always** a good idea if you do not qualify for tax credits anyway, or if your entitlement is going to be much smaller from now on.

And of course, if you spend the vouchers on **additional** childcare rather than just saving money on existing childcare, there will be no impact whatsoever on the childcare element of your claim and it will **always** be advantageous to accept them.

Despite the recent changes in the tax credit rules, there are still many higher-rate taxpayers who still qualify for them. They will save 42% in a salary sacrifice scheme rather than 32% (40% tax and 2% national insurance).

In certain cases it may even be worthwhile to come out of a salary sacrifice scheme and give up your childcare vouchers in exchange for a pay rise. Then you could take advantage of the fact that any increase in relevant income during the **current** year of claim is disregarded if it is less than £10,000.

That may well be advantageous if your children are about to start school and you don't need childminders any more. Bear in mind though that childcare vouchers can be used for many other things, even up to age 16, so you should consider that aspect too.

You also need to consider the new childcare vouchers scheme that is to be introduced by the Government in 2015 for all families where **both** parents work. This may be better for you than the current scheme which only operates through employers. More about this in the Bonus Chapter at the end of this book.

Chapter 29

Company Cars

At first sight, company cars might seem a rather unusual choice for a salary sacrifice scheme. After all, salary sacrifice schemes work by swapping salary for tax-free benefits, and as we all know, company cars are definitely not tax free!

Not many of them anyway. Electric cars will remain tax-free until 6th April 2015 and you only pay tax *on* 5% of the list price for cars with CO_2 emissions up to 75 g/km (8% for diesels) which includes many hybrid cars. This limit will go down to 50 g/km with effect from 6th April 2015 and the rate goes up to 7% in April 2016.

For all other company cars, however, you will pay tax on a benefit of between 10% and 37% of the list price, although the actual amount will depend on what rate of tax you pay (20%/40%/45%).

You are also taxed on any accessories that come with the car and for any private fuel paid by your employer.

So why is it so beneficial to have a company car in a salary sacrifice scheme? These car schemes are becoming quite popular because they offer the following five benefits:

- No employee national insurance on company cars
- Less tax on cars with low CO_2 emissions
- Trade discounts on large fleets
- VAT savings on leased cars
- VAT savings on maintenance costs

Employees can also benefit from all-inclusive packages that cover insurance and other running costs as well. Indeed, sometimes an employer can run a fleet of company cars more cheaply than its employees, so there is scope for cash savings there too.

For lower taxed cars, the employer may also achieve a national insurance saving. This can allow employers to offer their staff more expensive cars than would otherwise be the case.

Let's look at each of these factors in turn.

National Insurance

Salary earners currently pay 12% national insurance on all earnings between £7,755 and £41,450 and 2% above that. However, it does not apply to company cars or to most other benefits.

Therefore, a basic-rate taxpayer is immediately 12% better off with a company car. For higher-rate taxpayers the saving is only 2%, but this is still worth having combined with the other benefits.

However, the employer would still have to pay 13.8% class 1A national insurance on the taxable value of the car benefit, so no savings there.

Tax Savings on Low Emission Cars

The taxable value of a company car is usually calculated as follows:

List Price x Appropriate Percentage

The List Price is published by the manufacturer when the car is first released for sale in the UK. It is not the same as the price you would pay a dealer as that is normally discounted. The List Price is fixed for the entire life cycle of that make/model, so it is **never** adjusted for inflation, current market value or the age/condition of the individual vehicle.

The Appropriate Percentage is determined by CO_2 emissions and fuel type. You can look up the latest percentages on many websites including HMRC, the AA and various car manufacturers. Always add an extra 3% for diesels up to and including the 2015/16 tax year. However, the maximum percentage (including the extra 3%) can never be higher than 37%.

If the taxable benefit for the car is less than the salary sacrificed, you are saving tax.

For example, suppose you are a basic-rate taxpayer and sacrifice salary of £5,000 per annum in exchange for a petrol-fuelled car with a list price of £20,000 and CO_2 emissions of 136 g/km. For 2013/14 that car falls into the 19% band.

You will pay tax of £760 on the car (£20,000 x 19% x 20% tax), but you would have paid £1,600 tax and national insurance on £5,000 of salary (£5,000 x 32%). Therefore, you will save £840 this year.

If you are a higher-rate taxpayer, you will pay tax of £1,520 on the car (£20,000 x 19% x 40% tax), but you would have paid £2,100 tax and national insurance on £5,000 of salary (£5,000 x 42%). Therefore, you will save £580 this year.

However, you must also bear in mind that the taxable percentages for company cars tend to go up by 1-2% per annum. For a car with CO_2 emissions of 136 g/km, the percentage will be 20% in 2014/15, 22% in 2015/16 and 24% in 2016/17.

So the tax bill for basic-rate taxpayers will rise from £760 in 2013/14 to £800 in 2014/15 and eventually £960 in 2016/17. The tax bill for a higher-rate taxpayer will rise from £1,520 to £1,600 in 2014/15 and eventually £1,920 in 2016/17.

This is important to remember in cases where the tax saving is marginal as most company cars are leased for 3-4 years.

Trade Discounts

Most large fleet operators are able to negotiate big reductions in the cost of their cars – often around 25-30%. This saving can be passed onto the employees, thus enabling them to obtain much better cars than they would otherwise be able to afford. Alternatively they could sacrifice less salary.

For small employers it may not be possible to obtain any discount at all, and indeed some leasing companies charge a premium for smaller fleets to compensate for the fact that their admin costs per car are higher.

However, many leasing companies run salary sacrifice schemes on behalf of their clients and offer discounted rates, knowing that it is a new and growing market for company cars.

VAT Savings on Leased Cars

Normally it is not possible to recoup any VAT at all on the cost of a new car if there is any private use. For leased cars, however, it is possible to claim back 50% of the VAT charged on the rental if the owner is VAT registered and the car is used for business.

It does not matter how much business use there is. In theory you could drive the car to the Post Office once a year to buy stationery for the business and that would be sufficient to claim the 50%. In practice it would be wise to keep a mileage log in such cases.

Obviously this VAT saving is not available to private customers as they are not VAT registered. Therefore, if the employer rebates some or all of the VAT saving to the employees, it will allow them to sacrifice less salary and/or obtain a better car than they would have been able to otherwise afford.

VAT on Maintenance

Maintenance is one of the biggest costs of running a car and most garages charge VAT on both parts and labour. Even a mechanic who is not VAT registered would still bear VAT on the cost of the parts, which he would have to pass on to you. As most private owners are not VAT registered, it is not possible for them to recover this VAT.

However, a VAT registered employer can recover **all** VAT on maintenance costs provided there is at least some business use. There is no pro-rata reduction for private use of a company car as there would be for a sole trader. As with lease rentals, it does not matter how much business use there is, so a trip to the Post Office once a year would suffice.

The same applies to the maintenance contracts which often go with lease contracts. A VAT registered employer can recover 100% of the input tax on the monthly payments. This rebate can be passed on by the employer to offer a highly competitive remuneration package.

There is no VAT on insurance premiums or road tax so there are no equivalent savings there. There is also little scope for VAT savings on fuel due to the scale rates HMRC charge for private use.

It is possible to reimburse an employee solely for business mileage and claim the VAT back on that without a scale charge arising. However, the employer can do this anyway even if the employee drives his/her own car.

Also, it would be necessary for the employee to furnish receipts for fuel bills in order to allow a VAT recovery, and often these are neither kept nor received. For occasional business use, it is often more trouble than it is worth to claim back VAT on fuel/mileage.

Case Study
Low Emission Leased Car – Higher-Rate Taxpayer

Jim earns £60,000 a year and leases a Ford Focus 1.0 Edge for £250 a month with a maintenance contract of £30 a month (including VAT). He drives 1,500 business miles a year and claims the maximum tax-free rate of 45p per mile from his employer. His annual motoring costs (excluding fuel) are £370 for insurance, £20 for road tax (2013/14 rate) and £50 for breakdown cover.

He has a standard tax code of 944L so his net pay after tax and national insurance is £3,467.37 per month (2013/14 tax year).

His net annual income after running costs is as follows:

Net salary (£3,480.60 x 12)	£41,767
Business mileage (1,500 x 45p)	+£675
Lease rentals (£250 x 12)	-£3,000
Maintenance (£30 x 12)	-£360
Insurance	-£370
Road tax	-£20
Breakdown cover	-£50
Total	£38,642

His lease on the car is about to expire and he is wondering if he should join his employer's salary sacrifice scheme. For exactly the same type of car, he would be required to forego salary of £2,500 a year before tax and national insurance.

Jim would pay for no running costs except fuel, but could only claim 15p per mile for business mileage (the HMRC advisory fuel rate at 1 Sept 2013).

Other relevant information is as follows:

List price	£16,390
CO$_2$ emissions	109 g/km
Fuel type	Petrol
Taxable percentage	13% (2013/14 only)
Lease term	3 years
Lease rentals	£200 per month (inc VAT)
Maintenance	£24 per month (inc VAT)
Insurance	£300 per year (fleet policy)
Road tax	£20 per year (as before)
Breakdown cover	£30 per year (group policy)
Personal allowance	£9,440 per annum
NI primary threshold	£149 per week (employees)
NI secondary threshold	£148 per week (employers)
NI upper earnings limit	£797 per week (employees)
Income tax rate	40%
Employee NI rates	12% (2% above £797)
Class 1A NI rate	13.8%
Corporation tax rate	20%
VAT rate	20%

For simplicity, we will assume that all these figures remain the same over the three-year lease term apart from the taxable percentage. We already know that this will go up to 14% in 2014/15 and 16% in 2015/16. We will also assume that Jim's *notional* salary is frozen at £60,000.

Jim's financial position over the three years is as follows:

Net salary (£3,359.77 x 36)	£120,952
Less: Tax on benefit (£16,390 x 13% x 40%)	-£852
Less: Tax on benefit (£16,390 x 14% x 40%)	-£918
Less: Tax on benefit (£16,390 x 16% x 40%)	-£1,049
Business mileage (1,500 miles x 15p x 3)	+£675
Total over 3 years	£118,808
Annual equivalent (£118,808 / 3)	£39,603

So Jim gets an extra **£961** per year (£39,603 less £38,642). This is roughly equivalent to a 3% pay rise on his current salary of £60,000 (i.e. £1,657 less 42% tax and national insurance).

Now we must check that the employer does not lose out too much on the deal, otherwise it would not make economic sense. Without the salary sacrifice, its annual costs are as follows:

Gross salary	£60,000
Class 1A NI (£60,000-£7,696) x 13.8%	+£7,218
Business mileage (1,500 x 45p)	+£675
Total costs before tax	£67,893
Less: Corporation tax relief (£67,893 x 20%)	-£13,579
Total costs net of tax (per annum)	£54,314

Under the salary sacrifice arrangement, the employer's net costs over the whole three year lease term would be as follows:

Gross salary (£57,500 x 3)	£172,500
Class 1A NI (£57,500-£7,696) x 13.8% x 3	+£20,619
Business mileage (1,500 x 15p x 3)	+£675
Class 1A NI on car (£16,390 x 13% x 13.8%)	+£294
Class 1A NI on car (£16,390 x 14% x 13.8%)	+£316
Class 1A NI on car (£16,390 x 16% x 13.8%)	+£362
Lease rentals (£200 x 36)	+£7,200
Less: VAT on rentals (£7,200 x $1/6^{th}$ x 50%)	-£600
Maintenance (£24 x 36)	+£864
Less: VAT on maintenance (£864 x $1/6^{th}$)	-£144
Insurance (£300 x 3)	+£900
Road tax (£20 x 3)	+£60
Breakdown cover (£30 x 3)	+£90
Total over 3 years	£203,136
Less: Corporation tax relief (£203,136 x 20%)	-£40,627
Total costs net of tax	£162,509
Annual equivalent (£162,509 / 3)	£54,170

So the employer is benefiting also by £144 a year. When you add this to the extra £961 a year that Jim is getting, the overall saving under the scheme is **£1,105** per annum.

It might seem too good to be true that both Jim and his employer can save so much money when he is still driving the same type of car as before and the only real change is that his employer is paying for all the running costs (except fuel).

The first thing to note about this example is that the employer is passing on almost all of its gains to Jim by reducing the amount of salary he is required to forego. Not all employers will do this, and it is the main reason why Jim's net income is so much higher.

Secondly, the overall saving is driven mainly by the discount on the lease rentals. The employer obtains a 20% discount on the rates available to Jim, and there is a similar saving in the maintenance contract. Not all employers will be able to achieve a saving like this. It depends on the size of their fleet.

Thirdly, the employer also obtains healthy discounts in the cost of insurance and breakdown cover by running a fleet of cars. This spreads the risk and enables the employer to negotiate better terms. Again, these savings are not available to all employers.

However, the savings are much reduced as Jim is a higher-rate taxpayer and only saves national insurance at 2% rather than 12%.

The income tax saved is not very high in this example. This is because the taxable car benefit is not much less than the salary sacrificed, which has been kept down by the employer passing on most of its gains. Usually there would be a high tax saving on a car like this.

Corporation tax is only slightly affected because the employer is not making much profit out of the scheme.

You could regard this example as very much a "best case scenario" as far as higher-rate taxpayers are concerned. Not many will get a deal equivalent to a 3% pay rise, unless their employers can negotiate big discounts on the running costs of their cars and are willing to pass these on to their staff.

When Salary Sacrifice Will <u>NOT</u> Save You Money

Don't expect to save as much money as Jim unless:

- You drive a very "green" car
- Your employer can obtain huge discounts, and
- Your employer allows you to keep all of the gains

You should also note that these schemes work best for leased cars as the employer claims the lease rentals against tax immediately, whereas for "owned" cars it can only claim capital allowances.

They also do not work well for second-hand cars as tax on the benefit is based on List Price and therefore tends to be higher than the tax saved on the salary sacrifice, which is based on value.

Other Considerations

The Golden Seatbelt

Although most salary sacrifice schemes can be terminated after a year without cost, company car schemes are different in that leases tend to run for three or four years. If the lease does not run its full term there will be early termination charges.

Whilst your employer may be willing to pay these in the event of long-term illness, retirement, redundancy or maternity leave, it may be less inclined to do so if you just decide to up sticks and work for someone else instead.

You should not, therefore, enter into a salary sacrifice scheme for a company car unless you intend to commit to your employer for at least the duration of the lease, otherwise you may find yourself having to pay early termination charges.

Insurance

As your employer will be the legal owner of the car under a salary sacrifice scheme, they must take care of the insurance. Most will have a fleet policy which should work out cheaper for you, but remember that you may still have excesses to pay for any claims you make, or hire car charges whilst the car is off the road.

When you go back to insuring your own car again, you may also have some difficulty obtaining "proof of bonus" from the insurer, although your employer should be able to obtain the necessary document from them.

Maintenance

You should also bear in mind that most maintenance contracts exclude damage caused by the driver. Moreover, when the lease comes to an end, you must return the car in a reasonable state of repair, as determined by the BVRLA Fair Wear and Tear Guide. Any damage or excessive wear and tear, such as a small scuff on the bumper, will be re-charged by the lease company. Therefore, you will have to pay for any minor knocks or scrapes that you might have been prepared to live with if it was your own car. There may also be charges for excess mileage.

Inflation

One of the main advantages of having a company car is that you are immune to inflation (apart from fuel bills). Your salary might go up with cost of living increases, but the List Price of your car for tax purposes will remain fixed, if not the taxable percentage.

If your employer is paying for the insurance and maintenance, you are also shielded from any increases in those costs over the time you have the car. This is clearly beneficial when inflation is high.

Your Own Car

If you own a car outright, as opposed to leasing one, it will be more difficult to assess the financial benefit of a salary sacrifice scheme as there are no fixed monthly charges to compare it against.

Instead, you will have to work out the monthly average of all your motoring costs over a three-to-four year period, including depreciation and loan interest. You will need to estimate your future running costs, and also how much you can expect to sell the car for.

Fuel

As already mentioned, you can only claim the advisory fuel rates for business mileage in a company car (not the 45p rate) and they are always much lower, so you must factor this into the equation.

If your employer reimburses you too much, or you overstate your mileage claims, this could trigger a tax charge for private fuel, based on a deemed benefit of £21,100 per annum (2013/14 rate).

For a higher-rate taxpayer driving a car with a taxable percentage of 25%, this would result in a tax bill of £2,110 per annum – a high price to pay for just a few extra miles. This would not happen just for the occasional error though – only if it was habitual.

Capital Contributions

If a car is purchased by your employer rather than leased, you can reduce your tax bill by making a capital contribution of up to £5,000 towards the purchase price.

This is deductible from the List Price of the car and hence lowers the tax bill for each year that you drive it. Also, you get some of the money back when the car is sold by your employer, based on the proportion of the sale proceeds to the original cost.

Capital contributions tend to work better with cars that hold their value as you get more of your money back when the car is sold.

You may or may not gain from making a capital contribution, but even if you do not, it could entitle you to a better car than you would have had otherwise, or reduce the amount of salary you are required to sacrifice.

We must distinguish here between capital contributions and *personal use* contributions which also reduce your tax bill. With the latter, you are merely paying your employer £1 to save 40p tax, so you actually lose money that way.

Smoking

If you are a smoker, you may wish to check out your employer's policy on company cars, as they are considered to be part of the workplace when used for business purposes. They may have a policy requiring you not to smoke in it.

In theory, the no-smoking rule could apply to *any* car used for company business, even your own! However, in practice, you would only be breaking the law if you smoked whilst carrying passengers on a business trip, or if other employees drive the car too. If nobody ever uses the car but you, then it will be exempt.

Chapter 30

Salary Sacrifice:
Other Considerations

Salary sacrifice schemes generally work out quite well but there are several factors you should take into account before going ahead with one:

Final Salary Pensions

If you are lucky enough to have a final salary pension, joining a salary sacrifice scheme may not be advisable if you are approaching retirement age or expect to retire early due to ill health, as it could reduce your retirement benefits.

State Benefits

A salary sacrifice arrangement will reduce the amount of statutory maternity pay (SMP) you are entitled to, although this usually only reduces your SMP for the first six weeks. After that it reverts to a flat rate figure of £136.78 per week (for 2013/14) or 90% of your weekly pay if lower.

Similarly, there could be an impact on social security benefits such as income-related Employment Support Allowance, although most state benefits these days are means-tested.

Tax Credits

Childcare vouchers may reduce your tax credit entitlement (see Chapter 28). However, for other types of benefit, you could actually increase your entitlement with a salary sacrifice scheme, because your income will be lower.

With company cars, however, the benefit-in-kind may turn out to be higher than the salary sacrificed, particularly with diesels or high-emission cars.

You should also note that since 1ˢᵗ April 2012 any decrease in your relevant income of £2,500 or less is disregarded for your current year's tax credit claim.

Minimum Wage

Under no circumstances can a salary sacrifice scheme reduce your earnings below National Minimum Wage. Benefits-in-kind do not count towards the minimum wage. As NMW rates usually go up each year, you need to consider the future impact too.

Employment Contracts

The salary sacrifice will only work if your employment contract has been properly varied. If you remain legally entitled to the same salary as before, you will still be taxed on the old amount even if you happen to be paid less.

Disposable Income

It goes without saying that you should never reduce your disposable income to a level insufficient to maintain your standard of living, unless you have savings to fall back on. Reducing your tax bill is no good if you don't have enough cash to pay the bills.

Borrowing

Any salary reduction could affect your ability to borrow money, for example to buy a house or start a business. One solution is for your employer to provide the lender with an official letter confirming your pre-sacrifice reference salary.

For example, many University salary sacrifice documents state:

"You should quote your current annual salary on mortgage applications and your payslip will substantiate this figure as your annual salary. If The University Payroll Office receives requests for mortgage references from lenders they will quote your current salary i.e. before the reduction."

This issue can therefore be addressed. However, there is still a potential risk that some lenders will not accept your reference salary and insist on using the lower post-sacrifice salary.

Impact on Child Benefit

Your child benefit is gradually withdrawn if you or your spouse/partner earns more than £50,000 per year. If either person earns £60,000 or more, **all** the family's child benefit will be clawed back in higher tax bills.

A salary sacrifice scheme may help you reduce your income below £60,000 or £50,000 and thereby hang onto some or all of your child benefit (see Part 5).

Convincing Your Employer

Having convinced yourself that salary sacrifice is a good idea, your next task is to convince your employer. That may not be so easy!

Most big employers have dedicated HR departments who are paid to look into these matters and advise management on the best policy for both the company and the staff. Consequently, salary sacrifice schemes have had a large take-up in the corporate sector.

Smaller employers tend to rely on external advisers (e.g. solicitors and accountants) who may not be familiar with salary sacrifice.

If you work for a small firm there are several arguments you can use to convince your employer to introduce salary sacrifice:

- Other employers are doing these schemes
- They are approved by HM Revenue & Customs
- They are cheap and easy to administer
- They are a good incentive for key staff to stay
- They only have to run for a year so are not permanent
- Employees receive a **free** pay rise (no cost to the employer)
- The employer can benefit too from NI savings

If that doesn't work, then you could always look for another job!

Part 4

Tax-Free Expenses

Chapter 31

Introduction to Claiming Expenses

Expenses reimbursed by your employer are not always tax free. It depends on what your employer is reimbursing you for, how much and why.

Usually expenses will be tax free, but there are many traps for the unwary, both employers and employees, so it is worth knowing the rules.

There is a lot of legislation governing the payment of expenses, and most of the rules are summarised in HMRC Booklet 480, which also deals with employee benefits. This can be downloaded from the following page on the HMRC website:

www.hmrc.gov.uk/guidance/2012/480.pdf

HMRC Booklet 490 on Employee Travel is also well worth a read, and can be downloaded from here:

www.hmrc.gov.uk/helpsheets/490.pdf

In general, an employee's expenses are tax free if they are incurred *wholly, necessarily and exclusively* in the performance of his or her duties. That's a bit of a mouthful, so we shall henceforth refer to this requirement as "the basic rule".

It should be noted that expenses are not simply those incurred in the first instance by the employee and then reimbursed by the employer. They also include expenses paid by the employer where the employee enjoys a personal service, such as taxi fares, hotel accommodation or food and drink.

Thus, it is necessary for employers to review corporate credit cards and payments to suppliers as well as expense claims to determine the overall level of expenditure paid to or *on behalf of* employees.

Directors are also classified as employees for the purpose of these rules, something that often catches out self-employed people who set up their own limited companies after having been sole traders or partners previously. You may still be your own boss, but as far as the taxman is concerned, you are now merely a hired hand!

The Basic Rule

The basic rule for employee expenses is that they must be incurred *wholly, necessarily and exclusively* in the performance of your duties. But what exactly does this mean? Let's break this phrase down into its component parts:

Wholly

All of the expenditure that you incur on a particular item must be for the purpose of your job. For example, if you use your home telephone to make business calls, you can only claim for the business calls, not the line rental (which is your personal liability).

Necessarily

It must be absolutely necessary for you to incur the expense. For example, you cannot claim for the cost of a computer to work at home if you have one available at your normal place of work but simply choose to work at home instead occasionally.

Exclusively

There must be no other reason for you to incur the expense other than for the performance of your duties. For example, clothes are not generally tax free even if you have to wear certain garments for work, as they are also required for comfort and decency.

These are really tough conditions. Taken literally, it would be almost impossible for an employee to claim for anything. Fortunately, these rules are applied with a little common sense.

For example, food and drink are not exclusively for the purpose of performing your duties (unless you are a restaurant critic perhaps) but the taxman does allow you to claim subsistence if you are on a business trip or attending a temporary workplace. For travel and subsistence, the *wholly and exclusively* rule does not apply.

Also, you are allowed to make minimal private use of company equipment, such as computers, provided that the use is not significant and the equipment was purchased principally for use in the business.

The main thing you need to watch out for is any **dual purpose**. For example, if something was bought for both personal and business reasons, it would not be allowed as a tax-free expense.

This is the main difference between employee expenses and those incurred by the self-employed, who can claim a percentage of certain costs (e.g. cars) according to the degree of business use.

Tax Treatment of Expenses

So how are the rules applied in practice? The law is very clear. All expenses reimbursed in cash are taxable earnings. As such, they should be put through the payroll and treated as part of your pay. It is then up to you to claim the expenses back on your personal tax return if they satisfy the strict criteria.

However, the law does allow some alternative treatments. The following methods are approved by HMRC:

- Deduction
- Dispensation
- PAYE Settlement Agreement

There is an exemption for Mileage Allowance Payments up to the relevant tax-free limits. These do not have to be treated as part of your earnings, even without a dispensation.

We will now examine each of the above three methods in turn.

By Deduction

This means that the employer must add reimbursed expenses to your gross pay and then deduct any items considered tax free. This is the recommended method when the employer does not have a dispensation. Both the expenses and the deduction would be shown separately on your pay slip.

Consequently, if **all** your expenses are tax free, there will be no effect on your tax or net pay. However, if only some of them are deemed to be tax free, the balance will be subject to tax and national insurance as part of your pay.

In practice, this method is not used by many employers, in particular smaller ones who don't know the tax rules and simply assume that expenses incurred in the course of your duties should not go through the payroll at all.

Although that is technically wrong, it tends to be overlooked by the taxman provided the expenses really are tax free. Otherwise, the employer runs the risk of incurring a PAYE bill on them.

Dispensations

To avoid having to put tax-free expenses through the payroll or report them on P11Ds, the taxman can grant a dispensation to employers in respect of certain types of expenditure.

A dispensation is simply a letter setting out the type of expenses which do not have to be reported or treated as part of your pay. There will also be strict conditions on how the expenses are controlled in your employer's accounting system.

For example, it is likely that the expenses must be independently checked and approved, and that there are receipts for them. Also, expenses might only be covered by the dispensation in certain circumstances, such as on business trips.

An over-riding requirement for all dispensations is that the expenses do not give rise to a taxable benefit. Otherwise they must be treated by the employer in the normal way.

Also, they can never be used to exempt round sum allowances, even if those allowances are paid in lieu of expenses that are tax free in their own right. Round sum allowances must always go through the payroll.

It is quite possible for certain tax-free expenses to be specifically excluded from a dispensation if the taxman is not satisfied that your employer's accounting systems are up to scratch, or if there is insufficient scope for them to be independently verified.

A good example of this is business entertaining. Many small firms run by a sole director have to report these expenses on P11Ds if they are not covered by a dispensation, even if they are tax free.

The taxman always took the view that there could not be proper control over how much a sole director spent on entertaining his clients, or whether it even qualified as business entertainment. However, HMRC now seems more relaxed about such expenses being reviewed by an external adviser, such as an accountant.

A dispensation can be varied or revoked at any time, and is usually reviewed by HMRC at least once every five years. Therefore, it is important for the employer to adhere rigidly to the conditions.

PAYE Settlement Agreements

A PSA (as they are normally known) can be granted to an employer who wishes to pay tax on behalf of his employees for certain types of taxable benefit. This avoids the employer having to report them on P11Ds or for employees to declare them on their tax returns.

A good example of this is staff entertainment. If your employer is very generous, this can easily exceed the £150 per head exemption for annual functions (see Chapter 18), or for an event not to qualify as an annual function at all (such as a leaving party).

In that situation, it would normally be necessary for the employer to report the benefit on P11Ds, which would not go down very well with the staff. To avoid this, the employer can elect to report them on a PSA instead and pay the tax bill directly.

A PSA can be used to report the following types of expenditure:

- Minor items
- Irregular items
- Where it is impractical to operate PAYE

PSAs can be quite expensive for the employer as it is necessary to "gross up" the actual amount spent to determine the value on which tax must be paid. For example, an item costing £60 must be grossed up to £100 for a higher-rate taxpayer and the tax bill would be £40.

Employers must also pay national insurance at 13.8%. However, they do not have to pay class 1 national insurance contributions for the employee.

Examples of items that can be covered by a PSA are:

- Taxi fares and incidental travel costs
- Small gifts not covered by the "trivial items" exemption
- Occasional use of a holiday flat or a pool car
- Staff excursions, theatre trips, sporting events, etc

However, a PSA can never be used for cash payments, round sum allowances, shares or major benefits such as company cars, health insurance or beneficial loans. All these items should be taxed on the employee in the normal way.

Having said that, there have been reports in the media recently that senior civil servants are getting the tax on their company cars paid by their employers (effectively us) under PSA schemes. We wait with interest to see if this practice is allowed to continue.

Chapter 32

Travel Expenses

Disqualified Travel

The main rule is you cannot claim tax-free expenses for **ordinary commuting**, ie travel between your regular place of work and your home.

Unsurprisingly, private travel is not tax free either. For instance, you cannot claim for doing your shopping at lunchtime, even if you happen to buy goods for your employer at the same time.

Although home-to-work travel is prohibited, there are certain exceptions. The main one is necessary attendance at a **temporary workplace**.

The rules for temporary workplaces are very complicated and will be briefly summarised in the next section.

Travel **between workplaces** is also allowed as this takes place *during* the performance of your duties.

Business Trips

Business trips requiring an overnight stay away from home are covered, provided that business was the **main** reason for the trip. For example, you cannot book a holiday and then decide to combine it with a business trip, just for convenience.

If you set off on a business trip straight from home, without going to your normal place of work first, or go straight home afterwards, you can only claim travel costs (on a tax-free basis) if your journey is **substantially** different. If it is much the same as your usual journey, then it will not count.

The same goes for stopping off on the way home to see a customer or a supplier, or a colleague at another branch. This would not count, unless you had to make a substantial detour. It would need to be more than just one or two extra stops on the bus or train.

You would also need to prove that the appointment was absolutely **necessary** at that particular time in order for it to be tax free, as opposed to merely being personally convenient.

Travel between your home and work-related training courses run by your employer may or may not be tax free depending on where the courses are held. If they require a significant detour then they will be tax free, but not if your journey is much the same as usual.

More than One Permanent Workplace

It is possible to have more than one permanent workplace. For example, you could have two or more jobs. Travel between those jobs would not be tax free if the jobs are with different employers (unless they are within the same group of companies).

You could have more than one permanent workplace with the **same** employer, e.g. a maintenance engineer who visits several branches of the same firm on a regular basis. In a case like this, much depends upon the nature of the job and your specific duties.

For example, if you do pretty much the same type of work at each location and spread your time between them more or less equally, the likelihood is that they are all permanent workplaces. No home-to-work travel could be claimed on a tax-free basis.

However, if you visit a particular site for a specific task, such as a meeting or a safety check, it qualifies as a temporary workplace even if you go there fairly regularly. As such, home-to-work travel to/from that site can be claimed tax free so long as it is in a different location from your permanent workplace.

In some cases, your permanent workplace could be a specific geographical area. For example, a gamekeeper living and working on a country estate could treat the whole of that estate as a workplace, so home-to-work travel *within* the estate is tax free.

No Permanent Workplace

Sometimes an employee might have no permanent workplace at all. For example, a tree surgeon receiving orders by telephone and visiting customers all day could claim all of his travel against tax, including journeys to/from home.

On the other hand, if you regularly attend a depot to collect goods or receive orders, such as a bus garage or a maintenance yard, but do most of your work elsewhere, the depot would <u>not</u> be a temporary workplace, even if you never spend very long there.

Working at Home

Even if it is necessary for you to work at home sometimes, you cannot claim travel between home and a permanent workplace on a tax-free basis. This is because there is no *objective* requirement for the work to be done at home – it could be done anywhere.

However, if you are *obliged* by your employer to live in a particular location and also to work at home in order to do your job, travel between home and a permanent workplace would then qualify for tax relief. An area sales representative might thus qualify.

How Much You Can Claim

If your expenses are higher than the actual income you receive from that employment, tax relief is limited to the amount of your income. This is sometimes relevant for part-time jobs involving a lot of travel, such as a coach to a youth football team.

Obviously you can only claim tax relief on allowable travel expenses up to the actual cost that you incurred. If your employer chooses to pay you more than that, for example, the cost of a first class ticket when you only bought a second class ticket, then the excess will be taxable as earnings.

The reverse is also true. For example, if you choose to travel first class but your employer will only reimburse the second class fare, you can claim the excess as a deduction on your tax return. This will give you tax relief at your highest rate.

It should be noted that you do not always have to take the shortest possible route for your travel expenses to qualify for tax relief in full. For example, it may be quicker to take the M25 and drive around London rather than go through the city centre.

However, any significant detours for **private** reasons must be disallowed if they add substantially to your travel costs. Only if the additional costs were caused by a genuine error, such as getting lost or missing your stop, would the excess be tax free.

Working Abroad

There are special rules for people working abroad. Even if you attend a permanent workplace, your travel expenses (including those within the UK such as airport taxis) will be tax free if **all** the duties of that employment are performed outside the UK.

If you work overseas for **60 days** or more, you can also claim for visits by your spouse, civil partner or children, but you can only do this **twice** during the tax year (for each person visiting). It should be noted that this only covers the cost of visiting you *whilst* you are working overseas (or accompanying you to your place of work), not travel at other times or elsewhere.

Also, the special rules on foreign travel only apply to expenses reimbursed by your employer. If you bear the cost yourself, you cannot claim relief on your tax return. In this respect, the rules differ from the general rules for UK workplaces.

Disabled Employees

Employers are allowed to provide financial assistance tax free to disabled employees to help with the cost of getting to work, even if such travel is ordinary commuting. This rule applies even if the disabled person is capable of getting to work at no extra cost.

Also, the nature of the disability does not matter. Anyone who is disabled will qualify. HMRC do not have a formal definition of "disabled" but it would not include temporary disabilities such as a broken arm, or merely being old and frail.

Offshore Workers

Offshore oil and gas workers have to travel from the mainland to the rig, and employers often fly them out by helicopter. Strictly speaking this is ordinary commuting not covered by the special rules on overseas working, but sensibly there is an exemption for travel to or from the rig across the sea. It does not cover transport to or from the heliport though.

Late Night Taxis

The Government had intended to phase out this concession but had to backtrack as it would apparently have compromised the safety of certain "vulnerable groups". Therefore, you can still claim for taxis home after 9pm, subject to certain conditions.

The main condition is that working late must be **irregular**. It must not be part of your normal working hours. Hence shift workers do not qualify. This was one of the reasons why the Government wanted to ban tax relief for late night taxis. It was seen as unfair to lower paid workers who couldn't claim it.

It also excludes non-contractual overtime that tends to be predictable, or any late nights that you work from choice. It has to be overtime that you are *asked* to do by your employer.

Strictly speaking, this concession is only allowed when public transport has ceased or when it would be unreasonable to use it, for example when it would take you much longer than usual to get home. In practice this rule is interpreted very widely, at least by employers if not the taxman.

However, there is a limit to the taxman's generosity. You cannot claim for late night taxis (on a tax-free basis) more than 60 times during the tax year. Any extra would be disallowed.

Even this limit is very rarely allowed, as the rules have tightened up a lot recently. If you were to claim anything approaching this number of journeys for late night working, it would probably be challenged as regular rather than irregular.

The employer can, by arrangement with HMRC, pay the tax on behalf of the employee for any journeys that do not qualify.

Company Vans

Employees provided with a company van may be reimbursed for home-to-work travel, plus **insignificant private use**, without a taxable benefit arising. However, the reimbursement must not cover any other types of private use.

Insignificant private use means things like taking rubbish to the dump once a year, **not** doing the weekly shopping or dropping the kids off at school. It may be best to keep a mileage log for any such use, just in case the taxman should ever query your expenses.

Illustrative examples of all these rules (plus many more) can be found in *HMRC Booklet 490 – Employee Travel.*

Temporary Workplaces

We've referred to temporary workplaces quite a few times in this chapter. The concept is important because travel between your home and a temporary workplace is tax free.

But what exactly is a temporary workplace? Can you just assume that the phrase has its ordinary dictionary meaning?

Definitely not! The taxman has his own dictionary for terms like this, and it's a bit different from the one you or I would use. It certainly does not mean a place where you work temporarily, otherwise agency temps would always qualify.

A temporary workplace is somewhere that you go only to perform "a task of limited duration or for a temporary purpose". That's quite a mouthful, so let's examine what this phrase means in the taxman's parlance.

There are two main rules you need to be aware of and the good news is that you only have to satisfy one of them:

- The task must not take up more than 40% of your working time

- You must not **expect** to work more than 24 months at that location

If the task takes up less than 40% of your time but will last longer than 24 months, it may still qualify as a temporary workplace. Likewise, if it takes up more than 40% of your time but lasts for less than 24 months, it may still qualify as a temporary workplace.

Note the use of the word "may". It does not mean that it will definitely qualify as a temporary workplace, only that there is a chance it will. There are other hoops to jump through too!

For example, it will not be a temporary workplace if you attend it for all (or almost all) of the period that you are *likely* to hold (or continue to hold) the employment. For this reason, fixed term appointments or temporary agency jobs will not qualify.

The use of the word "likely" shows that it is the *expectation* that counts. You may not actually go on to work at any other location afterwards, but if it was expected at the outset that you would, it will remain a temporary workplace until it is clear that you will not work at another location.

The new workplace must require a **significant** change in your journey, or to the cost of that journey.

In *Booklet 490 on Employee Travel*, HMRC quotes the example of "The Square Mile" in London as an area that could be regarded as a single workplace. Moving from one part to another does not, in their view, require a significant enough change in your journey.

However, the word "location" is not defined in the legislation and therefore takes its normal dictionary meaning. Hence, it may well be worth challenging HMRC on this point in certain cases.

Temporary breaks count as part of the total length of time. This can have an unfortunate effect if you need to interrupt an assignment in order to work elsewhere for a short period. It could make an assignment last longer than the time actually spent on it, as the clock carries on ticking during your temporary absence.

The 40% Rule

The 40% rule also needs explaining as it is not as cut and dried as it sounds. It should be taken as an average of the total time spent on an assignment, rather than for any particular week or month.

For example, you may visit a branch once a week for a meeting on a regular basis (more than two years) and spend roughly the whole day there. That would be about 20% of your time, so it would count as a temporary workplace.

That would not change just because once a year you have to spend a whole month there (to manage a new project for instance). Over a whole year you would still only be spending 32% of your time there (ignoring holidays and other absences from work).

The 40% should be based on your total working hours, so if you work part-time the bar will be set lower. For example, if you work three days a week and spend 1.5 days at a particular place, that would be 50% of your total time, which is above the limit.

Always bear in mind that working somewhere **regularly** may still disqualify it from being a temporary workplace even if you spend less than 40% of your time there. The task must be of a temporary or self-contained nature.

For example, you would get away with going somewhere for a meeting or a safety check once a month, even though it is regular, provided it is the **only** reason you go there. The task is separate enough from the rest of your job to be clearly identifiable.

However, if you need to be at that place **generally** as part of your job, then it would not count as a temporary workplace even if you spend less than 40% of your time there. It would simply mean you have more than one permanent workplace.

In practice it can be difficult to distinguish between tasks that are self-contained and tasks that require your presence more generally. It would depend on whether or not you:

- Perform a significant part of your duties there
- Have an office, desk or support services at that location
- Perform similar tasks there to the place you usually work
- Carry out a number of different tasks at that location
- Can be expected by others to be *found* at that location

As you can see, temporary workplaces can get quite complicated!

Chapter 33

Subsistence

The rules on subsistence usually go hand in hand with the rules on travel. If you can claim tax-free travel then you can usually claim tax-free subsistence too. However, it must always be **reasonable**.

Whether it is reasonable or not depends on two things: cost and time. For example, if you spend half an hour meeting a client at the train station and bringing him to the office in a taxi, you cannot claim for your lunch as well. That would be considered excessive.

Likewise, if you go on a business trip, it would not usually be reasonable to claim for lunch in a *really* expensive restaurant, assuming that your employer would even allow this.

What do we mean by subsistence? Obviously it is food and drink, but only that necessary to *subsist* on. You cannot claim for luxury items such as fine wines or gourmet food. You may get away with this for business entertainment, but not for your own subsistence.

Alcoholic drinks are a grey area. If you are entitled to claim for lunch or dinner, then you can claim for beer or wine with your food, but you cannot claim subsistence for "liquid lunches" where the main source of nourishment is alcohol.

Also, you cannot turn a booze-up into a meal simply by ordering a bag of crisps or a sandwich. You could claim for the cost of the food and maybe one alcoholic drink per person, but not for the whole bar bill. Otherwise, it would become taxable earnings.

Normally you need to claim for the *exact* costs of subsistence, but the taxman recognises that this is excessive and unnecessary where there are many employees regularly claiming subsistence and the individual amounts are generally similar.

Therefore, employers have always been allowed to negotiate fixed daily rates for their staff based on the results of a sampling exercise. Provided they are engaged in qualifying travel, staff can be paid a daily allowance for their business trips.

The taxman has now extended this concession with a system of benchmark rates which all employers can now choose to adopt simply by ticking a box on Form P11D(X). These rates are based upon the length of time you are absent as follows:

One Meal Rate - £5
This may be paid when you have travelled on business for at least 5 hours and incurred the cost of one meal.

Two Meal Rate - £10
This may be paid when you have travelled on business for at least 10 hours and incurred the cost of one or more meals.

Breakfast Rate - £5
This may be paid when you leave home before 6am and this is earlier than usual. You must buy something to eat <u>after</u> your journey has started.

Late Evening Meal Rate - £10
This may be paid if you finish work after 8pm and this is later than usual. You must have worked your normal day and buy a meal <u>before</u> you get home.

You can claim up to **three** of the above rates in any 24-hour period, so in theory the maximum daily rate is £25. However, you can only claim for the breakfast or late evening meal rates in exceptional circumstances, not if it is a regular occurrence.

A meal is defined as any combination of food and drink but you must actually **buy** something. You cannot just bring a packed lunch with you. It does not matter how much you actually spend.

It must be stressed that these rates can only be claimed if you qualify for tax-free travel expenses, such as on a business trip or to a temporary workplace. You cannot claim them just because you've had a long day!

Also, the benchmark rates cannot be claimed if you stay overnight somewhere. Then you must claim the *actual* subsistence costs, which may well be considerably higher anyway.

The taxman is supposed to update these rates if the Consumer Price Index goes up more than 10%. The above rates have been in force since April 2009 so hopefully will increase soon.

Receipts

Receipts must always be kept for subsistence whether your employer uses the benchmark rates or not. Otherwise, it would be very difficult to prove that you bought a meal.

Where your employer reimburses the exact amount spent, the receipts would normally be attached to the expense claim and retained by your employer. In that case, you do not need to worry about them anymore.

However, where your employer pays you the benchmark rates, you may not be asked to furnish the receipts, at least not straight away. The whole point of the benchmark rates is to avoid individual receipts having to be checked for each and every claim.

This does not mean that you can throw them away once your employer has paid you. Employers are supposed to carry out regular checks on the operation of benchmark subsistence claims to ensure that all the rules are being followed. You may be asked to produce them at any time for a spot check.

Once your employer has confirmed that all checks have been carried out for the period in question, then you may throw receipts away. You will not be expected to keep them indefinitely.

Finally, HMRC publish tax-free scale rates for overseas business trips in local currency for individual countries. Your employer can choose to pay you these rates if it wishes. These include room rates for accommodation only, with subsistence claimed separately, or a 24 hour rate to cover all travelling expenses.

Importantly, if your employer does not reimburse the full amount of the subsistence actually incurred, you may claim the shortfall as a deduction on your tax return. However, if you choose to do this, it is advisable to keep the receipts in case there is a query.

Chapter 34

Hotels

If you are away from your normal place of work on a business trip and cannot reasonably be expected to return home that day, you are permitted to claim tax-free expenses for staying overnight at a hotel or other place of accommodation. After all, not even the taxman would expect you to sleep on a park bench!

However, the cost of the accommodation must be both reasonable and necessary. The first thing to note is that not everything on the hotel bill will necessarily be tax free. You are entitled to claim for the cost of the room and meals in the restaurant, but items such as laundry, phone calls home, drinks or newspapers are not covered.

In practice, you can claim 'scale rates' for incidental overnight costs such as these (more about this later) but the amounts are very small. The UK rate is just £5 per night and for overnight stays abroad it is £10 per night.

Other items on the bill may even be treated as taxable benefits if they go way beyond what is necessary for a business trip. For example, beauty treatments and spas are normally associated with holidays, not work.

However, you could claim for use of hotel internet facilities, conference rooms and phone calls if they were required for business purposes. Entertaining clients (actual or potential) in the bar or restaurant is also allowed if it is a genuine business occasion.

Reasonable

Costs must always be reasonable in order to be tax free. Of course, what is reasonable depends on many factors, such as the size and nature of your organisation, the length and purpose of your stay and, in particular, your personal circumstances.

As unfair as it might seem, a senior executive meeting important guests could probably claim a higher level of comfort than a salesman attending a seminar. It all depends on what would be regarded as the norm for your particular industry.

The taxman will always look first at whether other employees in your organisation regularly enjoy the same level of largesse when they are sent on business trips of similar purpose and duration.

For example, suppose you have just stayed at a posh five-star hotel with all costs met by your employer. The taxman (if it ever came to light) would ask if it is normal for your employer to do this and if not, why they did so on this particular occasion.

He will be looking for evidence that what you have actually received is a benefit-in-kind as a reward for doing your job well. In other words – a *de facto* bonus!

Necessary

The other condition is that the overnight accommodation must be necessary. If you are many miles from home on a business trip, finish work late and public transport has ceased, you would normally have a strong case for staying overnight at a hotel.

However, sometimes it may not be as clear-cut as that. As a real life example, I once had a client who entertained some of his business cronies at a top London hotel. The event went on until quite late, so he booked himself a room for the night at extortionate cost – on the company credit card of course.

However, he only lived in south London and could have got home in 20 minutes. I asked him why he didn't just jump in a taxi and go home. He explained that he didn't want to wake up his wife and kids, so he subjected himself to a night in a top hotel!

Commendable as that might have been, such noble sentiments cut no ice with the taxman. Family sensibilities like this are not recognised in the tax code. It wouldn't have been regarded as a *necessary* stay.

He might have got away with it if he had been hosting an ongoing event and had to be present in the morning to see to the guests. Even if that were the case though, it would have been difficult to justify as a *reasonable* cost.

Claiming hotel bills on your expenses is not always quite as straightforward as it seems. If you push the boat out too far, you could be letting yourself in for an unforeseen taxable benefit.

One last thing to note about hotel bills – they are tax free if public transport is disrupted due to strikes or other industrial action. However, the hotel must be at or near your place of work, and your stay must be only because of the industrial action.

Overnight Allowances

At the beginning of this chapter I mentioned that you can claim scale rates for incidental overnight expenses when you stay at a hotel or other place of accommodation during a business trip. The nightly rates are £5 in the UK and £10 outside the UK.

That may not sound very generous but they are only meant to cover minor expenses that you would otherwise be taxed on, such as laundry, newspapers, phone calls home or using the mini bar. They are not meant to cover more expensive items such as massages, manicures, or spa treatments. Indeed, these could even be taxable benefits if your employer reimburses the cost.

You can claim the scale rates whether or not you incur any extra costs on these items, but they are only tax free if your employer actually pays them to you or reimburses the cost of such items. You cannot claim them as deductions on your tax return.

If your employer does pay you the scale rates in full, you should make sure that any incidental non-business items on your hotel bill are deducted from your expense claim. Otherwise you would be getting paid for them twice and the expenses would be taxable.

Alternatively, your employer may prefer to just pay the whole bill, including extraneous items, or allow a higher scale rate. In that case, it would be necessary to compare the amounts reimbursed against the tax-free scale rates for the duration of your stay.

Any reimbursements above the scale rates are taxable in full, not just the excess. In that event, it is the **full** amount that will appear on your P11D. Payments up to the scale rates should not be reported on your P11D at all.

Alcoholic drinks purchased at hotels during business trips are often a source of confusion. Certainly, drinks bought at the public bar or from the mini-bar in your room are **not** tax free (unless covered by the benchmark rates or for genuine business entertaining).

However, drinks ordered with your meal are tax free provided the subsistence itself is allowable. This does not mean that you can have a skinful so long as there is a knife and fork in front of you. The amount spent on drinks must always be *reasonable*.

Fortunately, it is not necessary to go through your expenses and look at which costs were incurred on each separate day. You just need to add up the total for the duration of your stay. If it is within the scale rates for that period, then they are tax free.

For example, suppose you stay at a hotel for 5 days whilst visiting clients overseas and incur the following incidental costs:

Day 1
Phone calls - £4.20
Movie rental - £3.00
Mini-bar - £3.50
Total - £10.70

Day 2
Newspaper - £1.50
Gym session - £5.00
Total - £6.50

Day 3
Newspaper - £1.50
Phone calls – £2.70
Drinks at the bar - £8.40
Total - £12.60

Day 4
Newspaper - £1.50
Movie rental - £3.00
Mini-bar - £3.50
Total - £8.00

Day 5
Newspaper - £1.50
Laundry - £10.00
Total - £11.50

Overall total = £49.30

Scale rate - £10 x 5 days = £50.00

In this example, total expenses are within the scale rate for 5 days so they are not taxable, even though they exceeded the £10 limit on 3 separate days. Had they been just £1 higher, then the whole lot would theoretically have been taxable.

Chapter 35

Entertaining

Many senior employees are given entertaining budgets to lavish on actual or prospective business contacts. Generally, they can spend what they like so long as they stay within budget.

But what are the tax rules on entertaining expenses? Can you really flash the company credit card at will or claim back all your restaurant bills without any tax implications whatsoever?

The short answer is No. There are very strict rules about what is entertainment for tax purposes and what isn't. You must also consider **who** you are entertaining. For example, is it staff or customers? If it is the latter, are they from a foreign country?

You must be very careful with staff entertaining as technically this is taxable. True, there is an exemption of £150 per head for annual events, but spontaneous visits to the pub at lunch time or leaving parties do not qualify.

You may get away with the occasional working lunch in the office, but treating staff to a slap-up meal in a restaurant is definitely taxable. You can only get away with this on business trips or training courses well away from their usual place of work.

Fortunately, most large companies make arrangements with HMRC to pay the tax on staff entertaining directly, so no need to apportion the cost between employees. Otherwise, just imagine the arguments there would be over who drank the most wine, etc.

Business entertainment is different. This can never be a taxable benefit so long as it is a genuine business occasion. Basically, there has to be at least one external person present, although the overall numbers also matter.

For example, if you invite your external advisers to your Christmas party, that is not business entertainment. It is always the main purpose of the meeting that decides if it is a business event.

Another example – suppose 10 people from the same company go to a restaurant with just one client. It would be difficult (if not impossible) to pass that off as business entertaining as clearly it was a staff event. You have to play it by ear.

With business entertaining, there are always two questions to ask:

- What is the main purpose of the meeting?
- Why are other staff there?

Let's face it, many so-called business lunches are not for business reasons at all. They are just business associates from different organisations entertaining each other because they enjoy each other's company. Business matters may hardly be discussed at all.

This is what the taxman describes as "reciprocal entertaining" and it is disallowable. If he ever finds out, the cost would be treated as earnings and assessed on the person claiming the expenses or whoever's name is on the corporate card used to pay for the event.

But of course, it is virtually impossible for the taxman to police these rules. Who can say what the main purpose of a meeting was? After all, there is always some reason or other for business associates to meet up and discuss work-related matters.

In practice, it is up to employers themselves to curb such excesses. It may keep key staff happy and cement relationships with important customers, but other than that it is an unproductive use of their time and a drain on profits.

When the taxman visits for an employer compliance review, he is unlikely to focus much on individual expense claims (unless they are so huge they stick out like a sore thumb). He will look instead at the overall picture for that organisation.

If the level of business entertaining is abnormally high, or there are regular meetings with the same people for no apparent reason, or lax internal controls over expense claims, then it is likely that the taxman will make further inquiries.

How can you protect yourself from awkward questions over your entertaining expenses, not just from the taxman but from your own boss? As an accountant, I always advise my clients to keep a detailed log of their business entertaining.

For example, you should log a) who was there, b) the purpose of the meeting, c) where you went, and d) what was discussed.

It may be a pain, but it will stop the taxman in his tracks if you can prove, beyond dispute, that it was a proper business meeting.

The other question concerns staff. Obviously someone from your organisation needs to be present or it wouldn't be entertaining, but you can't bring a whole posse along. Otherwise it would compromise the main purpose of the meeting.

The cost of food and drink consumed by staff is deemed to be *incidental* to the main purpose of business entertaining (if that is what it is). In other words, the costs attributable to staff are only incurred because they are required to be there.

Consequently, you cannot apportion the cost of an event between business entertaining and staff entertaining (or subsistence). It is either one or the other. For this reason, staff should ideally only attend a business entertaining event if there is a demonstrable need for them to be present.

Of course, this should be easy enough to prove in most cases. It is often necessary (or at least desirable) for suppliers or customers to meet the staff they deal with on a day-to-day basis and get to know them in informal surroundings.

You just need to be sensible about it and not bring so many that it turns into a staff party rather than a meeting to discuss business. It may be wise to schedule a meeting in advance rather than arrange it spontaneously on the day, so there is email evidence that the main purpose was indeed business related.

Just because a meeting is for business doesn't mean you are not allowed to talk about anything else. So long as that is the main purpose, and business is indeed discussed, you could spend most of the time yakking about the football results (if the boss lets you).

There is often confusion about whether staff from other group companies qualify as external for business entertaining. The general rule is that they do, provided the companies deal with each other on an arm's-length basis.

However, if one company in a group re-charges the cost of entertaining staff from other group companies, it is likely that the company employing those staff would have to treat it as staff entertaining, with consequent PAYE implications.

Lastly, I referred to the entertainment of foreigners earlier. This is only usually relevant for VAT purposes, as the employer is allowed to re-claim the input tax in some cases. It has no effect on whether it is tax free or not.

Chapter 36

Working from Home

Modern technology makes it much easier for people to work from home. With the right equipment, software and telecom links, you may not really need to be in the office to do your job.

This could save you time and commuting costs (and you won't need to shave or put on make up or wear a suit!) Your employers could save money too because the company's overheads will be reduced (i.e., it can use a smaller office).

But what about the tax position? Can your employer pay anything towards your household expenses? Can you claim anything on your tax return as a deduction? Usually the short answer is No.

As an employee, all expenses must be incurred wholly, exclusively and necessarily for your job in order to be tax free. Household bills are normally ruled out automatically as you would have to pay them anyway.

However, the taxman recognises that there are certain extra costs that cannot be itemised, such as wear and tear of furniture and carpets. For this reason, he very generously allows £4 per week as a tax-free allowance for people working at home!

Not a huge sum admittedly, but then again how much extra do you really pay for working at home? Your gas and electricity bills may be higher, but that's about it. In fact, you probably save more money in train fares or petrol.

Claims for gas and electricity may be possible but you would need to keep very good records showing the costs both before and after you started working at home. As many bills are estimated and fuel costs go up all the time anyway, this may be difficult to prove.

The £4 per week is not automatic. It is only allowed if you have an ongoing **arrangement** with your employer to work at home. You can't claim it unilaterally just because you *prefer* to work at home, but you can volunteer for a home working arrangement.

You don't need to work at home every day, but there must be a regular pattern, not just the odd day here and there. Also, your employer must actually pay you this allowance for it to be tax free. You can't just claim it as a deduction on your tax return.

Telephone and Internet Bills

Working at home often involves making calls on your own telephone, whether it's a fixed landline or mobile. You may also have to use your own internet connection.

Can you claim anything from your employer towards these costs? Only if you have itemised bills and you can identify which calls were for business. Given that most phone calls only cost pennies, it is hardly worth the time and trouble of adding them all up.

Sadly it is not possible to claim anything from your employer towards the line rental or the monthly tariff, at least not tax free. As far as the taxman is concerned, these are your personal bills that you would have had to pay anyway.

If your employer does contribute anything towards the fixed costs, it must be treated as earnings and put through the payroll. It may still be worthwhile but you will have to pay tax and national insurance on the amount paid by your employer.

The only exception is if a line is installed **solely** for business purposes. In that case, you could claim the whole bill as an employment cost on your tax return. However, there would have to be no private use of the phone whatsoever.

If the contract is in the name of your employer you have a bit more leeway. The bills can then be paid by the employer (or reimbursed) tax free so long as any private use is insignificant.

It would also be wise for your employer to put a clause in your employment contract that all private use of the phone must be logged and reported. At least that will prove it is a legal obligation, even if no such calls are ever logged.

Mobile phones are tax free anyway if the contract is in the name of the employer. You can make as many private calls on them as you like, provided only one mobile is available for personal use.

If your employer installs an ADSL link in your home so you can access his systems remotely, it is usually self-evident that it is required solely for business. The same goes for home-workers who need a phone to do their job, such as customer support staff.

In that event, there will be no taxable benefit provided personal use is insignificant. It will not need to be reported on P11Ds.

The same cannot be said if your employer pays for your personal internet connection, or makes a contribution towards it. As far as the taxman is concerned, this is your personal liability and you would have had to pay the bills anyway.

It does not matter how much business use you make of it. If the bills are no higher than they would have been anyway, you are not out of pocket so any contributions by your employer will be taxable and should go through the payroll.

For the self-employed it is different. They are not subject to the strict rules on employee expenses, so they can claim a fair proportion of telephone and internet bills against business profits on their tax returns.

Chapter 37

Occupational Allowances

You might think that the tax rules would be the same for everyone as regards expenses, but that would be too simple. In fact, there is a whole raft of tax-free allowances for particular occupations.

For example, nurses (including midwives) are allowed to claim £12 a year for shoes and £6 a year for stockings or tights when the colour or style is obligatory (male nurses can claim for socks too) as a deduction on their tax returns.

Airline pilots can claim a tax-free £850 per annum to cover items such as watches, suitcases, torches, pens, sunglasses and irons as a deduction on their tax returns. Any contributions from their employers are deducted from the tax-free amount. This limit has been fixed since 2006/7 so is getting a bit out-of-date now.

Long-distance lorry drivers can claim £34.90 per night tax-free to meet the costs of accommodation and subsistence for the year ended 31 December 2013. However, those that sleep in their cabs can only claim 75% of this amount.

Note this only applies if their employers actually reimburse these costs to them, not as a deduction on their tax returns, so there is no tax relief if the drivers bear the cost themselves.

PE teachers can claim for training shoes and tracksuits, even if they occasionally wear them outside school in other sporting activities. However, they cannot claim for towels, T-shirts or other items not recognisable as sports equipment if used outside school.

There are also a number of **Working Rule Agreements** that have been agreed with HMRC by employer federations such as the Joint Council for the Building and Civil Engineering Industry. These lay down precise rules for travel and subsistence expenses.

The agreements specify tax-free rates for particular industries and require workers to sign statements confirming that they comply with the tax rules, such as not working permanently at the site they are getting the allowance for.

The Working Rule rates are OK if workers share rooms or stay in caravans but are usually too low otherwise. If an employer wishes to pay above the tax-free rates, they can obtain a dispensation from HMRC for a higher amount. However, this will mean getting their workers to furnish receipts, which is usually no easy task!

A full alphabetical list of Working Rule Agreements can be found on the HMRC website on the following pages:

www.hmrc.gov.uk/manuals/eimanual/   followed by:

eim50000.htm   Agricultural workers to census takers

eim60000.htm   Clergy/ministers of religion to journalists

eim65799.htm   Local authority officials to Royal Observer Corps

eim70199.htm   Seafarers to waiters

Part 5

How to Protect Your Child Benefit

Chapter 38

Child Benefit Basics

Child benefit is an extremely valuable tax-free gift from the Government to parents. Those who qualify currently receive the following annual payments in 2013/14:

- £1,055.60 for the first child
- £696.80 for each subsequent child

Depending on the number of children, a family can expect to receive the following total child benefit payment:

Children	Total Child Benefit
1	£1,056
2	£1,752
3	£2,449
4	£3,146

plus £696.80 for each additional child.

Child benefit generally continues to be paid until your children are 16 years old. The payments will continue until age 20 if the child is enrolled in full-time 'non-advanced' education, eg GCSEs, A levels and Scottish Highers. Degrees do not qualify.

The Child Benefit Charge

Child benefit is withdrawn from 'high earners' through the levying of a new tax called the High Income Child Benefit Charge. It generally kicks in where one parent has income over £50,000 and the maximum charge is payable if income is above £60,000.

By income we mean "adjusted net income", which generally includes all your taxable income less certain deductions such as pension contributions.

When it comes to calculating the child benefit charge, we are only interested in the **spouse/partner with the biggest income**. The couple's total income does not matter.

TABLE 2
TABLE 2
Child Benefit Charge 2013/14

Income	1 Child			2 Children			3 Children		
	CB	Tax	Net	CB	Tax	Net	CB	Tax	Net
50,000	1,056	0	1,056	1,752	0	1,752	2,449	0	2,449
51,000	1,056	105	951	1,752	175	1,577	2,449	244	2,205
52,000	1,056	211	845	1,752	350	1,402	2,449	489	1,960
53,000	1,056	316	740	1,752	525	1,227	2,449	734	1,715
54,000	1,056	422	634	1,752	700	1,052	2,449	979	1,470
55,000	1,056	528	528	1,752	876	876	2,449	1,224	1,225
56,000	1,056	633	423	1,752	1,051	701	2,449	1,469	980
57,000	1,056	739	317	1,752	1,226	526	2,449	1,714	735
58,000	1,056	844	212	1,752	1,401	351	2,449	1,959	490
59,000	1,056	950	106	1,752	1,576	176	2,449	2,204	245
60,000+	1,056	1,056	0	1,752	1,752	0	2,449	2,449	0

Notes
1. Income is adjusted net income of highest earner
2. CB is the maximum annual child benefit
3. Tax is the child benefit charge
4. Net is the amount of child benefit left over after paying the charge

Calculating the Child Benefit Charge

For every £100 of income over £50,000 a tax charge equivalent to 1% of the child benefit is levied on the highest earner in the household. As a result, if the highest earner has income of £60,000 or more, the tax charge will be 100% of the child benefit claimed.

If your income is somewhere in the £50,000-£60,000 bracket, the simplest way to calculate the tax charge is to divide the amount above £50,000 by 100 and treat that as the percentage claw-back:

Example 1

Paula has income of £53,000 and receives child benefit of £1,752. She is the highest earner in her household. The excess over £50,000 is £3,000. Divided by 100 we get 30. Paula's tax charge is 30% of her child benefit, ie £525 (rounded down to the nearest whole pound).

Example 2

John has income of £53,550 and his wife receives child benefit of £1,752. He is the highest earner in the household. The excess over £50,000 is £3,550. Divided by 100 we get 35 (rounded down to the nearest whole percentage). John's tax charge is 35% of the child benefit, ie £613 (rounded down to the nearest whole pound).

Table 2 contains some sample child tax charges for the 2013/14 tax year and shows how much child benefit you will have left after paying the tax. Note the Net column falls to zero at £60,000.

Eye-watering Tax Rates

If you are the highest earner in your household, you may face a triple tax whammy on income in the £50,000-£60,000 bracket:

- Income tax
- National insurance
- Child benefit charge

Hence you could face a sky-high tax rate on some of your income:

Example

Robert has income of £50,000 and is the father of two young children. He is the highest earner in the household. He receives a £10,000 salary increase at the start of the 2013/14 tax year.

How much tax will he pay on this extra income? As a higher-rate taxpayer he will pay 40% income tax and 2% national insurance: £4,200. Because his income is £60,000 he also faces a 100% child benefit charge: £1,752 for two children. His total additional tax is £5,952, i.e. almost 60% of his pay rise goes in tax.

TABLE 3
Marginal Tax Rates: £50,000-£60,000

2013/14 Tax Year

Children	Earnings*	Rent/Interest	Dividends
1	53%	51%	37%
2	60%	58%	44%
3	66%	64%	52%
4	73%	71%	60%
+	7%	7%	8%

* Earnings include salary income and self-employment profits
+ Extra tax payable for each additional child

Table 3 lists the marginal tax rates payable on different types of income that fall into the £50,000-£60,000 bracket.

Clearly, the more children you have the higher your marginal tax rate. For example, if your income for 2013/14 lies somewhere between £50,000 and £60,000, and you have four children, you will pay 73% tax on all earnings in the £50,000-£60,000 bracket.

Chapter 39

Protecting Child Benefit: Pension Contributions

One of the simplest ways for salary earners to avoid the child benefit charge is by making pension contributions.

Pension contributions reduce your adjusted net income, which reduces the child benefit charge. If your adjusted net income ends up below £50,000, you will avoid the child benefit charge altogether.

Pension contributions also provide income tax relief and, sometimes, national insurance relief too (see Chapter 27).

Example

Peter earns a salary of £60,000. His wife earns £30,000 and receives child benefit for two children: £1,752.

Peter invests £8,000 in a self-invested personal pension (SIPP). The taxman will add £2,000 of basic-rate tax relief to his pension pot producing a total gross pension contribution is £10,000.

Peter also receives £2,000 of higher-rate tax relief (found by multiplying his £10,000 gross contribution by 20%).

Peter's £10,000 gross pension contribution will result in his adjusted net income falling from £60,000 to £50,000. This means he will completely avoid the child benefit charge of £1,752.

In summary, Peter enjoys total tax relief of £5,752 (58%) on his £10,000 pension contribution:

- £2,000 basic-rate relief
- £2,000 higher-rate relief
- £1,752 child benefit charge

If Peter doesn't make any pension contributions, he faces paying £4,000 income tax on the top £10,000 slice of his income, and the maximum child benefit charge: £1,752. Peter's total tax on this income will be £5,752, leaving him with just £4,248.

Peter has to decide whether he wants £10,000 saved in a pension versus £4,248 of after-tax income to spend. Many would agree that making pension contributions is worthwhile when the tax relief is so high.

Pension Tax Relief Rates

Peter enjoys 58% tax relief because he has two children. If you have fewer children or more children you will enjoy a different amount of tax relief on your pension contributions:

No. Children	Tax Relief 2013/14
1	51%
2	58%
3	64%
4	71%

Note: Assumes adjusted net income in £50,000-£60,000 bracket both before and after making the pension contribution.

The more children you have the more tax relief you will enjoy. However, even those with just one child will enjoy over 50% tax relief. Most higher-rate taxpayers only enjoy 40% tax relief on their pension contributions.

Bigger than Normal Pension Contributions

Those in the £50,000-£60,000 income bracket should consider making bigger than normal pension contributions from 2013/14 onwards.

This strategy makes most sense if you expect your income to rise above £60,000 in the near future or if your children are approaching the age where child benefit will be withdrawn.

For example, let's say you wouldn't normally make a gross pension contribution of more than £5,000 but decide to double it to

£10,000 in 2013/14 to take advantage of the 58% tax relief available (two children).

You could then suspend making pension contributions in 2014/15, for example if your income rises from £60,000 to £65,000. A £5,000 pension contribution in 2014/15 would attract just 40% tax relief, compared with the 58% available in 2013/14.

Small Pension Contribution

Is it worth making a small pension contribution if you can't afford the maximum required to completely avoid the child benefit charge? Yes, because you will still enjoy the high rate of tax relief.

Example

Aaron earns £60,000 and invests £800 in his pension. The taxman tops this up with £200 of basic-rate tax relief for a gross pension contribution of £1,000. Aaron will also receive £200 in higher-rate tax relief (£1,000 x 20%). The gross pension contribution of £1,000 reduces his adjusted net income from £60,000 to £59,000. This reduces the child benefit charge by 10%, ie £175. Aaron's total tax relief on his £1,000 gross pension contribution is £575, ie 58%.

Postponing Pension Contributions

As a general rule it can make sense for basic-rate taxpayers (ie those earning less than £41,450 in 2013/14) to postpone making pension contributions until they become higher-rate taxpayers. Higher-rate taxpayers enjoy 40% tax relief on their contributions, whereas basic-rate taxpayers only receive 20% tax relief.

Some higher-rate taxpayers should also consider postponing pension contributions in order to enjoy more tax relief in the future.

For example, if your income in 2013/14 is somewhere between £41,450 and £50,000 you could consider postponing pension contributions if you expect your income to be in the £50,000-£60,000 income bracket in the near future.

Example

Saul has income of £50,000 in 2013/14. His wife receives child benefit for two children: £1,752. His income does not exceed £50,000 so he does not have to pay the child benefit charge. If he makes a gross pension contribution of, say, £5,000, he will enjoy just 40% tax relief.

Let's say he expects to have taxable income of £60,000 during the next 2014/15 tax year. So instead of making a £5,000 pension contribution in 2013/14 and a £5,000 contribution in 2014/15 he makes a £10,000 pension contribution in 2014/15.

By doing this he will enjoy 58% instead of 40% tax relief on the postponed pension contribution.

One Person Makes the Pension Contributions

Generally, where one spouse is a higher-rate taxpayer and the other is a basic-rate taxpayer, tax relief may be maximised by getting the higher-rate taxpayer to make all the pension contributions. Why? Because 40% tax relief is better than 20% tax relief.

With the introduction of the child benefit charge, the same tactic can be used by couples who are *both* higher-rate taxpayers. Where one spouse/partner is in the £50,000-£60,000 income bracket, and the other has a smaller income, it may be worth getting the higher earner to make all the family's pension contributions, even for just one or two tax years.

Example

Chris and Maria are both higher-rate taxpayers earning £60,000 and £50,000 respectively. They claim child benefit for two children: £1,752. In the past they've each made pension contributions of £5,000 and have enjoyed 40% tax relief.

In 2013/14 the couple decide that Maria should stop her pension contributions and Chris should increase his by £5,000 to £10,000. By making an additional £5,000 pension contribution Chris will avoid an additional 50% child benefit charge, saving the couple £876.

Both Partners Earn £50,000-£60,000

Where both partners are in the £50,000-£60,000 bracket, the most tax-efficient strategy is to *equalise* their adjusted net incomes.

Example

Alistair earns £58,000, his wife Wilma earns £55,000. The couple want to make a £5,000 gross pension contribution in 2013/14. If Alistair makes the entire contribution this will take his adjusted net income to £53,000. Wilma will then become the household's highest earner with £55,000, resulting in a 50% child benefit charge.

The best solution may be for Alistair to make a £4,000 gross pension contribution, with Wilma making a £1,000 gross contribution. They will both then have adjusted net income of £54,000 and an additional 10% of their child benefit will be retained (£1,000/£100 = 10).

Income over £60,000

Even those with income *over* £60,000 can enjoy above-average tax relief by making bigger than normal pension contributions.

Example

Colin has earnings of £65,000 in 2013/14. His wife earns £30,000 and receives child benefit for three children: £2,449. On the top £15,000 slice of his income, Colin faces an £8,749 tax charge: £6,300 income tax and national insurance and a £2,449 child benefit charge.

If Colin makes a gross pension contribution of £5,000 he will enjoy 40% tax relief. He will not avoid any of the child benefit charge because his adjusted net income will not fall below £60,000.

Fortunately his aunt Doris left him some money in her will so Colin decides to make a £15,000 gross pension contribution in 2013/14 and then stop making contributions for a year or two. Colin's pension contribution attracts £6,000 income tax relief and, by reducing his adjusted net income to £50,000, allows him to entirely avoid the £2,449 child benefit charge. The total tax relief is £8,449 or 56% of his gross pension contribution.

TABLE 4
Tax Relief 2013/14: Income over £60,000

		No. Children				
Income	**Pension**	**1**	**2**	**3**	**4**	**5**
£60,000	£10,000	51%	58%	64%	71%	78%
£65,000	£15,000	47%	52%	56%	61%	66%
£70,000	£20,000	45%	49%	52%	56%	59%
£75,000	£25,000	44%	47%	50%	53%	55%
£80,000	£30,000	44%	46%	48%	50%	53%

Notes
1. Income: Adjusted net income of highest earner before making pension contribution
2. Pension: Gross pension contribution required to take adjusted net income to £50,000

Obviously the higher your income the bigger the pension contribution you have to make to get your income below £60,000 and ultimately down to £50,000.

However, for some individuals, including those with income well over £60,000, the tax relief may make it worthwhile.

Table 4 shows the tax relief available to a high earner who makes a pension contribution big enough to take adjusted net income down to £50,000.

For example, if your taxable income is £75,000 and you have four children, a £25,000 gross pension contribution will be required to take your adjusted net income to £50,000 and completely avoid the child benefit charge.

However, you may decide that this is worth doing, perhaps just the once, because you will enjoy 53% tax relief.

Dangers

When it comes to postponing or accelerating pension contributions there are potential dangers. For example, the Government could reduce the tax relief on pension contributions. This could harm anyone who puts off their contributions.

Summary

- **Income £50,000-£60,000**. Consider making bigger than normal pension contributions from the start of the 2013/14 tax year. Then make smaller contributions when your income rises above £60,000.

- **Income under £50,000**. Consider *postponing* pension contributions and making bigger ones when your income is in the £50,000-£60,000 bracket. You can invest your savings in an ISA in the meantime.

- **Income over £60,000**. Consider making bigger than normal pension contributions if you can reduce your adjusted net income to £50,000 and avoid the child benefit charge. The higher your income the more difficult this becomes. The more children you have the more attractive this strategy becomes.

Chapter 40

Protecting Child Benefit:
Other Techniques

The best tax-saving strategy is to make pension contributions if this will take your adjusted net income below £60,000.

Other tax-saving techniques include:

- Salary sacrifice arrangements
- Deferring bonuses
- Reducing working hours

Salary Sacrifice Pensions

Employees can benefit from salary sacrifice pensions, which are the most tax efficient of all. Salary sacrifice pensions provide both income tax relief and national insurance relief.

Example

Mark has a salary of £60,000 in 2013/14 and is the highest earner in a household claiming child benefit of £2,449 for three children. On the top £10,000 slice of income he pays 42% income tax and national insurance and a child benefit charge of £2,449. Total tax: £6,649, leaving him with a paltry £3,351. His employer also pays 13.8% national insurance on this income: £1,380.

Mark's employer offers a salary sacrifice pension arrangement, so Mark decides to sacrifice £10,000 of salary and, in return, his employer contributes £10,000 to Mark's pension. The employer also pays in the £1,380 national insurance saving (there is no national insurance on employer pension contributions).

Mark's adjusted net income is now £50,000 so he avoids the child benefit charge. The end result is he has £11,380 in his pension instead of just £3,351 of after-tax salary.

Essentially Mark has an £11,380 pension contribution that has cost him just £3,351 with the taxman forking out the remaining £8,029.

The tax relief is a whopping 71%! In other words, the taxman will pay for 71% of your retirement saving if you have three children and your income lies in the £50,000-£60,000 bracket.

The following is the amount of tax relief other parents can enjoy:

Children	1	2	3	4
Tax relief	58%	64%	71%	77%

Year-end Pension Planning

The normal salary sacrifice rule is that the arrangement should last at least a year. However, with salary sacrifice pensions it is not necessary to stipulate a period for which the arrangement must be entered into.

This may be of help to employees who want to do some year-end tax planning to avoid the child benefit charge.

For example, in January 2014 you may realise that, if you receive your normal February and March pay cheques, you will pay the maximum child benefit charge.

With the agreement of your employer you may decide to reduce your salary for the two months (but not below the level of the national minimum wage), with matching pension contributions made by your employer.

Your salary could then be restored to its previous level at the start of the new tax year.

Childcare Vouchers

It is possible to sacrifice some of your salary in exchange for childcare vouchers. These will save you income tax and national insurance and, by reducing your income, may help you reduce the child benefit charge.

The basic idea is that the employer gives the employee a childcare voucher. The employee gives the voucher to a childcare provider. The child carer then redeems the voucher to receive payment.

For higher-rate taxpayers who joined schemes after 5th April 2011, the tax-free amount is limited to £28 per week or £1,484 per year.

The tax-free limit applies per parent, not per child. In other words, if you have three children the maximum annual exemption is still £1,484 per year per parent.

However, if you have several children the small reduction in your income may produce a hefty reduction in the child benefit charge:

Example

Guy earns £55,000 and is the highest earner in the family. His wife Tumi receives child benefit of £3,146 for four children.

Guy sacrifices £1,484 of salary in exchange for childcare vouchers. This will save him £623 in income tax and national insurance (£1,484 x 42%).

The reduction in his income to £53,516 will also result in him paying a child benefit charge of 35% instead of a 50%. Additional saving: £472.

As with all salary sacrifices, the scheme must be structured correctly. For example, the employee's employment contract must be changed correctly, the childcare voucher scheme must be open to all employees and the childcare must be provided by a registered child carer.

Deferring Cash Bonuses

It may be possible to avoid the child benefit charge by deferring cash bonuses.

Example

Rory, a father of three young children, expects to receive a salary of £50,000 and a bonus of £10,000 in 2013/14. As things stand he faces the maximum child benefit charge: £2,449.

With his employer's consent, his bonus is not payable until 2014/15. This means Rory's adjusted net income in 2013/14 will be £50,000 so he will avoid the child benefit charge and save £2,449 in tax.

It may be possible to repeat this 'roller-coaster' income strategy, taking below-average income during some tax years and above-average income in other years. In years of below-average income it may be possible to reduce the child benefit charge.

Problems with Deferring Bonuses

Deferring bonuses is not necessarily straightforward. For starters, it will require your employer's co-operation. Your employer may not be happy to postpone your bonus if this means his tax deduction for the payment is also postponed. Secondly, HMRC may seek to tax the bonus in year 1, even if it is only paid in year 2.

There are different rules for discretionary and contractual bonuses. If the bonus is discretionary it will only become taxable when your employer exercises his discretion and awards it. Contractual bonuses are generally calculated according to a set formula or conditions. To change a contractual bonus it will be necessary to properly change the terms of your contract *before* you actually become entitled to receive the payment.

It is generally more difficult for directors to defer cash bonuses than it is for other employees.

Professional advice should be obtained to ensure the bonus is taxed in the correct tax year.

Reducing Working Hours

In some cases it may be beneficial to work less and spend more time with your children:

Example

Libby, a mother with three children, earns £52,000 (£1,000 per week) and is the highest earner in the family.

On the top £2,000 slice of income she pays £840 income tax and national insurance and a £489 child benefit charge. After tax she is left with just £671.

She pays a childminder £4 per child per hour for 40 hours which adds up to £480 per week.

Libby asks her employer if she can sacrifice £2,000 of salary in exchange for two additional weeks' leave during the summer holidays. Her employer agrees because the business is going through a quiet patch.

The end result? Libby loses £671 of income but saves £960 of childminder fees. Total saving: £289. Plus she gets two extra weeks with her children.

Part 6

Personal Service Companies

Chapter 41

Introduction

Not many people knew what a personal service company was until quite recently, when it was reported that various top civil servants and BBC executives were using them to save tax.

Since then personal service companies have had rather negative connotations in the eyes of the media and public, an impression that politicians have done little to dispel. However, the truth is somewhat different.

Yes, some high-ranking individuals and the organisations they work for have used personal service companies solely to save tax and national insurance. But for thousands of other people they are an efficient, flexible and sometimes even a necessary way of earning a living.

What Are Personal Service Companies?

Typically, they are limited companies that are owned and managed by a single person who will be the sole director, shareholder and employee. That person will own 100% of the share capital, usually just a single ordinary share of £1.

You can get partnerships or companies owned by two or more people (who may have joined forces to save on administrative costs) that also serve the same purpose. Generally speaking, however, a personal service company is a one-man band.

Also, as the name suggests, a personal service company can only exist if the owner is selling his/her own services. If you are selling goods or the services of other people (e.g. your employees) you are not running a personal service company. It must be a vehicle for your own hard work, whether it is by your brain, brawn or both.

Even this does not fully describe a personal service company, otherwise a whole host of professional firms like solicitors, accountants or even hairdressers would fall under this description.

Just because you work on your own through a company does not necessarily make it a personal service company. A personal service company only exists if you tend to work for one client at a time, e.g. a contractor on a temporary assignment.

If you work for the public at large, or even just for 3-4 regular clients on a rotating or simultaneous basis, then you are not running a personal service company (at least not in the usual sense of the word) but a real business with multiple clients.

Why Do Personal Service Companies Exist?

The demand is driven chiefly by organisations anxious to keep people off their payrolls. For instance, why recruit employees to do a one-off piece of work, such as a large IT project? A whole army of workers may be needed for the duration of the project but the business may have no need for them afterwards.

Of course, the business could always hire workers on a temporary basis, either directly or through an agency. There is nothing to stop an employer stipulating that a contract will only run for six months or a year, after which the worker will leave with no redundancy pay.

However, such workers would still be employees, either of the agency or the business and, as such, they may enjoy all sorts of rights they would not enjoy if they were self-employed (e.g. holiday pay, unfair dismissal, maternity leave, etc).

This brings us to the other key driver of demand for personal service companies – the desire to avoid being caught by employment legislation. As we all know, employee rights have grown significantly in recent years. Auto-enrolment into workplace pension schemes is just the latest burden on employers.

Employers also have to pay national insurance at the eye-watering rate of 13.8%. Not for nothing has this been described as a tax on jobs. It is a major disincentive to hiring.

Employer's national insurance can be removed from the equation altogether if there is no employment relationship in the first place, for example if the worker is self-employed and pays tax directly to HMRC. You might think that most businesses would prefer this.

Unfortunately, the PAYE rules deter employers from hiring workers in this way because legally it is their duty to operate PAYE on the earnings of all individuals who should be classified as employees. If they get it wrong, they could end up with a huge PAYE bill.

It is not a matter of personal choice whether you are employed or self-employed. It depends on the *kind* of working relationship you have, and that is a notoriously grey area. Even if the worker insists that he/she is self-employed, the taxman may decide otherwise.

For this reason, many businesses shy away from hiring people on a self-employed basis and insist that they work through their own companies. That way, all the tax risk is with the worker (under the IR35 rules which are discussed in Chapter 44).

True, there are many freelancers who do not work through their own companies but they tend to be more common in sectors such as advertising where there is a tradition of freelancing and hirers believe, rightly or wrongly, that there are no PAYE issues.

The other reason for the growth of personal service companies in recent years is that people are more willing and able to use them. This has been driven by both economic and regulatory changes.

It is much cheaper and easier to run your own company now than it used to be many years ago. For one thing there is no longer a requirement for an expensive annual audit. Most small companies are exempt, which saves them thousands of pounds every year.

Also, it costs less than £20 to set up a company these days, and it can be done online almost immediately. Business banking is much cheaper now too with internet accounts.

The trend has been encouraged by changes in the labour market. Working patterns have been transformed in recent decades and the labour market is much more flexible now than it used to be.

Employment law has also become much more onerous, resulting in hirers and agencies encouraging (or even insisting upon) the use of companies by contractors.

Finally, we should not downplay the tax-planning angle. As we shall see, there are ways to save tax and national insurance using a company, and people are much more aware of this now.

Chapter 42

How Do Companies Save You Tax?

Not all personal service companies can be used to save tax. If you are caught by the IR35 rules (see Chapter 44) the amount of tax and national insurance you can save is very limited indeed. However, if you can avoid IR35, the picture is very different.

If you run a personal service company you are both a director and a shareholder. You have the power to decide how much salary you take from the company and may not even be obliged to pay yourself the national minimum wage.

As a director you are deemed to be an office holder rather than an employee, and fees paid to office holders are not within the scope of the minimum wage, even though they are subject to PAYE.

Therefore, you can take as much or as little salary as you like. You can even take no salary at all if you wish. However, most company directors opt to take a small salary because it is tax efficient and protects their state pension entitlement.

As a shareholder you can also receive dividends. Most people running a personal service company take dividends in preference to salary. Why? Because there is no national insurance on dividends. They count as investment income, not earnings.

This saves you not just 12% employee's national insurance but also 13.8% employer's national insurance. If you took salary instead, you would pay total national insurance of 25.8%.

This is one reason why companies are so tax efficient. It's not so much tax you save but rather national insurance. With national insurance rates at record highs now, this is well worth doing.

Dividends also carry a tax credit which means most of the tax is paid by the company, not the shareholder. You only pay tax on UK dividends if you are a higher-rate taxpayer.

Lastly, you may be able to save or defer tax by retaining profits in the company and extracting them in future years instead.

Case Study

In this case study we'll compare the total tax and national insurance (NI) payable (2013/14 rates) for three different scenarios:

- Case 1 - Employee paying tax and NI under PAYE
- Case 2 - Freelancer working on a self-employed basis
- Case 3 - Contractor using personal service company

	Case 1 Employee	Case 2 Freelancer	Case 3 Contractor
Gross income	£50,000	£50,000	£50,000
Basic rate tax	£6,402	£6,402	£0
Higher rate tax	£3,420	£3,420	£866
Corporation tax	£0	£0	£8,461
Class 1 NI	£4,214	£0	£0
Class 2 NI	£0	£140	£0
Class 4 NI	£0	£3,204	£0
Total tax & NI	£14,036	£13,166	£9,327
Net income	£35,964	£36,834	£40,673
% gross income	72%	74%	81%

How the Contractor's Tax is Calculated

For Case 3 it is assumed that the contractor takes a tax-free salary of £7,696 from his company. This amount of salary is completely tax free because it is below the various income tax and national insurance thresholds (see Chapter 1).

The salary is a tax-deductible expense for the company, which means its taxable profits are £42,304 (£50,000 less £7,696). The company pays corporation tax at 20%, so its tax bill is £8,461.

The company is now left with after-tax profits of £33,843 which can be paid out as dividends. There is no national insurance payable on dividends, nor is there any basic-rate income tax.

This is to prevent double taxation because dividends are paid out of profits that have already been subjected to 20% corporation tax.

Higher-rate tax is, however, payable on dividends at an effective rate of 22.5% on the *gross* amount. Gross dividends are calculated by dividing cash dividends by 0.9. So in this example the gross dividends are £37,603.

Adding together the salary of £7,696 and the gross dividends of £37,603 the contractor has total taxable income of £45,299.

The amount of dividend income over the higher-rate threshold is £3,849 (£45,299 less £41,450) so total income tax at 22.5% is £866.

Overall Savings

The client also saves employer's national insurance of £5,838 under Cases 2 and 3. If this saving was passed on (in whole or in part) to the self-employed freelancer or the contractor, their net incomes would be even higher.

You can see here that the employee and freelancer pay the same income tax but the self-employed freelancer pays less national insurance (9% versus 12%). The contractor does best of all because he pays no national insurance whatsoever.

The contractor also pays £495 less tax than the employee or the freelancer, giving him a total saving over the employee of £4,709, even without negotiating a higher fee. There is clearly a huge financial advantage to working through a company.

It might seem counter-intuitive that the contractor saves tax as well as national insurance since the tax rates are the same for both the company and the three individuals. Why does this happen?

It is due to the fact that corporation tax shields some of his income from higher-rate tax, thus effectively increasing the higher rate threshold by £4,219. This saves tax (at 20%) of £844.

There is also a tax loss to the contractor as he wastes some of his personal allowance on dividends, which do not incur basic-rate tax anyway. This loss comes to £349 (£9,440 less £7,696 = £1,744 x 20%). Therefore, his net gain is only £495 (£844 less £349).

In reality, the contractor would aim to use up his whole personal allowance with bank interest or other earnings, not dividends.

Chapter 43

Splitting Income with Your Spouse or Partner

There is another way that contractors can save tax, and that is by splitting the dividends with a spouse (or civil partner) who is not a higher-rate taxpayer. This means giving them shares in the company and then paying dividends on those shares.

The last Labour Government took a very dim view of this. HMRC tried to use legislation already on the statute book to challenge such dividends as *settlements* by one spouse on the other, on the grounds that they were far in excess of the recipient spouse's economic contribution to the business.

Basically, if the courts found that the shares were no more than a "right to income" and the dividends were "bounteous" then they could be taxed on the other spouse instead, usually at higher rates.

This potentially affected almost every husband and wife company in the country and flew in the face of established tax planning. If the taxman got his way, many thousands of married couples could have been landed with huge tax bills going back several years.

The issue was finally resolved with the famous **Arctic Systems** case (Jones v Garnett) which first began legal life in 2004 and, after many twists and turns through the courts, went all the way up to the House of Lords in July 2007.

The Lords ruled in the taxpayer's favour on the grounds that:

- The share owned by Mrs Jones was an *outright* gift from her husband (despite the fact that she subscribed £1 for it), and

- It was not "wholly or substantially a right to income" as the shares conferred other ownership privileges (e.g. voting rights) as well as dividends.

Hence, although there was indeed a settlement, it was exempt as a gift between spouses.

Gifts between spouses cannot be challenged by the taxman as settlements, even if the spouse receiving dividends does little or no work for them, provided they are a) an outright gift with no strings attached, and b) ordinary shares with full voting rights.

Unmarried Couples and Other Family Members

Although spouses and civil partners are in the clear, what is the position for unmarried couples and other family members? After all, there is no gifts exemption for them.

Good news and bad news on this front. The bad news is that the settlor will almost certainly have a retained interest if the couple live together and the dividends go into a joint account or are otherwise used to pay household expenses, etc.

The good news is that the settlements legislation only deems the settlor to have a retained interest in the case of married couples and civil partners. There is no legal presumption of this for unmarried couples.

Hence, unmarried couples can avoid a retained interest by keeping their finances completely separate. If they live together, the dividends received by the non-earning partner should be paid to an account in his/her own name and not spent on the household.

For family members who live apart and are not minor children or dependants of the settlor, it should be relatively simple to prove that there is no retained interest. For most family businesses, therefore, the settlements legislation should not be a problem.

Latest Position on Income Splitting

The Labour Government did attempt to introduce new tax rules to prevent so-called income splitting following the Arctic Systems case, but they were found to be totally unworkable, and since then the issue has remained firmly on the political back-burner.

The reason it was so difficult to introduce income-splitting rules is that it is almost impossible to define what the true market rate for a spouse's contribution actually is in a typical family business. It would be a constantly moving target and totally subjective.

It is most unlikely that the Government will try to interfere again with the allocation of business profits between spouses or civil partners, either through a company or a partnership. To do so, they would have to remove the gifts exemption in the settlements legislation, which would have other far-reaching consequences.

However, although there are no official plans to prevent dividend splitting, it is still possible to fall foul of the settlements legislation if you are not careful about how you do it. To avoid this, always remember the following rules:

No Alphabet Shares

These are shares of different classes, e.g. Class A, B, C, etc. The only reason for having them is to distinguish between the classes in some way, and there is a danger that some classes may lack voting rights or other privileges of ownership. Consequently there is a risk that they may become wholly or substantially a right to income, thereby falling foul of the settlements legislation.

No Preference Shares

These are definitely out, as they confer no rights on the holder apart from the specified coupon rate. Hence they are not exempt as a gift between spouses as they are merely a right to income. That was the decision in the 1996 tax case of Young v Pearce.

No Payment for Shares

It is vitally important that the shares are a gift between husband and wife. Ideally, therefore, the spouse should not pay for them. It is also preferable if the shares are transferred from one spouse to the other rather than subscribed for in a new share issue.

No Conditions

The shares must be an *outright* gift. There must be no conditions along the lines of gifting them back on demand at some future date, nor should there be any other strings attached, for example that the income must be used to pay household bills.

No Joint Accounts

This is only for unmarried couples as it helps to avoid any suggestion of a retained interest by the settlor. Spouses and civil partners can use joint accounts for their dividends as they are shielded by the gifts exemption even if there is a retained interest.

No Dividend Waivers

Again this is not absolutely ruled out. Dividends waivers can be a useful tax-planning strategy sometimes, but they could potentially be treated as a settlement in certain circumstances, so take care.

Spouse Wages

It is also possible to pay your partner a small salary for work such as secretarial or IT support, but it must not be excessive otherwise it could be disallowed by the taxman as a trading expense. A small salary could be tax efficient if your partner has no other source of income as it will use up their tax-free personal allowance.

Where spouse wages might be challenged by the taxman, it is best to keep some type of evidence such as a job description, a log of the work actually done or time sheets. It goes without saying that you must actually pay them for the work done!

Some people like to make their spouse Company Secretary and pay them an annual fee just for holding that office. However, this is only worth about £300 a year as that is all a registrar would charge for a full secretarial service, including registered office.

Case Study

We will now look at how much tax a contractor may be able to save by splitting dividends and paying a small salary to his partner.

Tom is an IT contractor and works for various clients through his own company, Tom Tech Limited. His wife stays at home to look after their children and has no other income. She spends about 10 hours a week providing back-office support for the business.

None of his contracts are caught by IR35 (see Chapter 44) and all of the company's profits are distributed as salary and dividend. He has no other income. How much tax could he save if he gifts 50% of the shares to his wife and pays her a salary of £7,696 per year?

	Before	After
Gross income	£100,000	£100,000
Corporation tax	£18,461	£16,922
Income tax	£10,866	£1,732
Total tax	£29,327	£18,654
Net income	£70,673	£81,346
Net % of gross	71%	81%

Tom and his wife save an additional £10,673 per year. He does this by making use of his wife's personal allowance and basic-rate tax band. This is in addition to the tax and national insurance savings he already makes by working through a personal service company.

Only £3,464 of his cash dividends are exposed to higher-rate tax, compared with £48,294 before he split his income with his wife. He also saves £1,539 in corporation tax by paying his wife a salary. At just £16 per hour for a 48-week year, her salary should not be challenged as excessive.

As an added bonus, neither spouse earns more than £50,000 a year so they get to hold on to all of their child benefit too.

Of course, you should never enter into arrangements like this with your spouse unless you are both comfortable with them. It goes without saying that you should both trust each other, as once the shares have been gifted you cannot expect to get them back again!

Splitting dividends with your spouse (or civil partner) obviously works better at higher income levels as the whole point is to save higher-rate tax. However, there is a limit beyond which no further tax savings are possible using this method.

This limit changes every year with the new tax and national insurance thresholds.

The following table shows how much can be saved at various income levels with a 50/50 split of the shares based on 2013/14 rates and allowances.

Gross Income	Tax/NI Before	Tax/NI After	Tax/NI Saved	Marginal Saving	Rate of Saving
£40,000	£6,461	£4,922	£1,539	-	-
£45,670	£7,595	£6,056	£1,539	£0	0%
£50,000	£9,327	£6,922	£2,405	£866	20%
£60,000	£13,327	£8,922	£4,405	£2,000	20%
£70,000	£17,327	£10,922	£6,405	£2,000	20%
£80,000	£21,327	£12,922	£8,405	£2,000	20%
£90,000	£25,327	£14,922	£10,405	£2,000	20%
£91,340	£25,863	£15,190	£10,673	£268	20%
£100,000	£29,327	£18,654	£10,673	£0	0%

There are two trigger points in this table – £45,670 and £91,340. Up to £45,670 no gain is achieved by splitting dividends as there is no higher-rate tax to pay at that level of income anyway. The only gain is a flat £1,539 which comes from paying the spouse a salary of £7,696 and utilising his/her personal allowance.

From that point onwards, you save 20% by splitting dividends as you are avoiding higher-rate tax on the additional income. This is, of course, the difference between 40% and 20% tax.

This constant rate of saving ceases abruptly at £91,340 (i.e. double the effective higher rate threshold of £45,670). Above that level of income there is no further gain to be made by splitting dividends.

This table is based on a 50/50 split of dividends and annual salaries of £7,696 each. It also assumes that neither spouse has any other income that would distort the figures.

In reality, it is highly likely that one or both spouses will have other income to take into consideration. In that case, a different split of shares would be required to optimise the tax savings.

Gifting shares to your spouse is a fairly informal process. All you need is a Stock Transfer Form (or equivalent) and an entry in your Register of Members (which all companies are supposed to keep). However, to prove it was done, it may be wise to get it witnessed.

Chapter 44

IR35

The History of IR35

Any contractor working through their own company will be familiar with IR35. It has been the bane of their lives ever since it was first introduced in April 2000.

The IR35 tax rules must be given serious consideration by anyone working through a personal service company – ignore them at your peril!

IR35 was the name given to a 1999 Budget press release in which the Government announced its intention to introduce new tax rules to counteract the use of 'intermediaries' (e.g. personal service companies and partnerships) to avoid tax and national insurance. The name stuck and everyone now refers to IR35, even HMRC.

Basically, IR35 is a set of rules whereby people working though their own companies or partnerships may be taxed as though they were employed directly by the end client. In other words, the taxman looks *through* the intermediary as if it didn't exist.

You'll notice I used the words "may be taxed", not "will be taxed". That's because the rules don't apply to everyone. The IR35 rules are only supposed to affect people who would have been employees of the end client were it not for the existence of the intermediary.

This is where IR35 gets fuzzy. How do we know if a director of his/her company would have been an employee were it not for the company? The line between employment and self-employment has always been blurred, and today it is blurrier than ever.

In fact, it is a myth that you have to prove you are self-employed in order to avoid IR35. All you have to do is prove you would **not** have been an employee. It may seem the same but there is a subtle difference. It is far easier to prove the latter than the former.

IR35 relies on case law to distinguish between those who are caught by the rules and those who are not. There is no statutory definition of self-employment to go by. This means each case must be judged on its own merits and looked at in the round.

At one extreme are the so-called Friday to Monday workers, who are employees one week and then suddenly turn into contractors doing exactly the same job the next week. Almost certainly, they are caught by IR35 and by law should comply with those rules.

At the other extreme are consultants who operate through a personal service company and work directly for the client but are running a genuine business and satisfy all the usual criteria for self-employment. In between are thousands of other people, each case different from the next.

If the Government had restricted IR35 to the most blatant cases and made the employers/clients responsible for compliance, then perhaps IR35 could have been a successful piece of legislation. Unfortunately, it was far too ambitious in scope and too woolly.

No one really knew for certain who was affected by IR35. It hung like the sword of Damocles over every personal service company contractor, who had to decide whether to pay massive amounts of tax and national insurance, perhaps unnecessarily, or run the risk of being caught years later, with huge financial repercussions.

Not only that, but the original IR35 proposals were changed to put the onus to comply on contractors rather than the clients. All the ingredients were there for one of the most unworkable pieces of legislation ever to hit the statute book.

It did have one good effect though which is often overlooked. Back in the late 1990s, there were a lot of personal service companies being set up by former employees (Fridays to Mondays) and it wasn't all totally voluntary.

A lot of arm twisting was going on by unscrupulous employers trying to make their organisations leaner and fitter by reducing headcount, thus making them more attractive to potential buyers. Consequently, the staff concerned lost their employment rights.

IR35 did a lot to discourage this sort of thing (but not completely as the risk of non-compliance is with the contractor rather than the erstwhile employer). It also undoubtedly had a deterrent effect, especially in the early days when people were more uncertain about it.

A whole new industry sprang up around IR35 specialising in contract reviews, insurance, tax investigations, tribunal cases and advisory services. It was also the catalyst for the creation of a new trade association, the Professional Contractors Group, which was formed to fight IR35 and defend the interests of its members.

Over the years, a long series of IR35 cases followed in the courts and the tax tribunals. Some issues were clarified, while on others the waters were muddied still further.

Enough cases were won for contractors to become fairly confident about their IR35 status on the whole. All the same though, it has been a constant source of worry for most ever since it was enacted.

When IR35 Applies

For IR35 to bite there has to be a *relevant engagement* between the intermediary company and the client. A relevant engagement is one which would have been a contract of employment were it not for the existence of the intermediary company.

Early case law introduced the concept of a *hypothetical contract*. This is the contract that would have existed if the worker had been engaged directly by the client rather than the intermediary. Would this contract have been one of employment or self-employment?

To answer that question, it is necessary to refer to case law going right back to the *Ready Mixed Concrete* case in 1968. This case set out a number of factors that are necessary in order for an employment relationship to exist.

The factors you are looking for to win an IR35 case are as follows:

- Being able to control the work
- Lack of any mutuality of obligations
- The right to appoint a substitute
- The scope to make efficiency gains
- Having some financial risk
- Use of your own equipment

- The ability to work at home
- The ability to work your own hours
- An obligation to rectify work at no cost
- Not being part and parcel of the organisation
- The extent to which you operate as a business

The first three on this list are by far the most important. Any one of these would be a magic bullet killing IR35 stone dead if it can be found to exist. An employment contract simply cannot exist if any of those three factors are present.

Unfortunately, they can also be the hardest to prove. It is not always easy to show that any one of these factors exists simply by looking at the contract. The whole working relationship must be evaluated to see how it operates in practice.

Therefore, it is very important to ensure that the terms of your contract reflect reality and do not exist only on paper. Otherwise, the courts would simply disregard them.

Control of the work includes when, where and how a job is done. Being able to control **how** you do the work is by far the most important. Having to work set hours on-site does not on its own give the client control of the work.

Basically, to show control you would have to prove that the client's manager was merely reviewing your work and not asking you to do it a different way, or switching you to another task instead. In practice, this is a very grey area.

Control of the work is usually divided between the client and the contractor. It is rare to have complete control, especially on a project where a number of people are involved. Also, the client may still have a *right* of control, even if it is not exercised.

Mutuality of obligations (or MOO as it is shortened to) is basically the obligation of the employer to provide work and pay the employee for the duration of the contract and the obligation of the employee to do that work.

If the worker can decide whether he wants to do that work or not, **or** the hirer can suspend or dispense with the services of the worker without giving any notice as and when he pleases, then it is highly unlikely that MOO exists.

Contracts of fixed durations are indicative of MOO, whereas contracts that end when the task in hand is complete tend to exclude MOO. To avoid IR35, you are aiming for the latter.

The right of substitution is also rarely cut and dried. In practice, a client would probably want to vet anyone you delegated your work to. On its own this would not be a problem, provided they did not have the final say. A substitution clause must give you an **unfettered** right to send someone in your place.

In practice, a substitution clause would probably allow the client to check out the new person but not to unreasonably deny you the right to appoint him if he was suitably qualified and experienced. Also, it is not necessary for the right of substitution to have been exercised for it to be effective. It merely needs to be unfettered.

If none of these three factors are present, it does not automatically follow that a contract is caught by IR35. The other factors may well be sufficient to defeat IR35 on their own. The courts will always look at a contract in the round and weigh up all factors together, rather than adopt any kind of scoring system.

In particular, the scope to make efficiency gains can be important. This will exist when you charge a fixed fee for a job and complete it sooner than expected. Efficiency gains are rarely achievable if you charge a daily or hourly rate based on your attendance.

Financial risk will exist if there is a fair chance that you will not be paid for your work, or you incur unexpected costs. For example, the client may be unable to pay your bill due to cash-flow problems, or you may incur higher research costs than anticipated.

The ability to work at home whenever you want or to work your own hours may also be important factors in IR35 cases, as not many employees are able to do this. It depends on the nature of the work more than anything else.

Having to rectify defective work at your own cost is another pointer towards self-employment, as few employees could be made to do so unless they were being paid by their output. A clause like this would have to be seen as capable of being exercised.

Being part and parcel of an organisation includes things like having your own office on their premises, recruiting their staff, taking part in the social activities of the firm or having business cards in the firm's name. This is indicative of employment and is best avoided if you wish to remain outside the scope of IR35.

As for operating like a business, this will include having your own website, taking out insurance, advertising your company, employing staff, renting business premises, issuing your own contracts and working for other clients at the same time.

None of these things have any direct relevance in their own right as IR35 applies to individual contracts, not to the company itself. However, if you do operate as a proper business, it makes it less likely that IR35 will apply to any one contract.

In an IR35 investigation, HMRC will always ask to see the contract with the client. This may sometimes be with an agency, in which case they will ask to see your own contract with the agency too. In some cases, it may not even be obvious who your client actually is.

The focus then will be on whether the contracts actually reflect the working arrangements. For this reason, standard contacts can be risky as they may not reflect commercial reality, especially if the client would not stand by certain clauses were they to be invoked.

How IR35 Works

The only clear thing about IR35 is how tax and national insurance are actually calculated if a contract is caught by the rules. This is prescribed by the legislation and follows a laid down procedure:

Step 1
Add up all income and benefits received by the intermediary from relevant engagements during the tax year and deduct 5%.

Step 2
Add up all income and benefits received directly by the worker for relevant engagements not already taxed as employment income.

Step 3
Deduct any allowable expenses met by the intermediary that would have been tax free if the worker had been employed by the client, such as travel and subsistence whilst attending a temporary workplace or professional subscriptions.

161

Step 4
Deduct any capital allowances that the worker would have been entitled to if employed by the client.

Step 5
Deduct any pension contributions to approved schemes made by the intermediary on behalf of the worker.

Step 6
Deduct any employer's national insurance paid by the intermediary for the year in respect of the worker.

Step 7
Deduct any salary or benefits paid to the worker during the year by the intermediary as employment income.

Step 8
Calculate the employer national insurance element of the running total left after Step 7 and deduct this to find the "Deemed Employment Payment".

This figure is then treated as if it was a bonus paid to you by your own company at the end of the tax year and subjected to PAYE accordingly.

There are a few points worth making about this calculation.

Firstly, IR35 is on a *received* basis, so you only count fees that were actually paid by the end of the tax year. In other words, do not count debtors or unbilled fees.

You should also only include fees from relevant engagements, so exclude contracts outside IR35. In theory, you may have some that were caught by IR35 and some that were not, although in practice that would be rather unusual.

Next, there is a 5% allowance within Step 1 which is meant to cover all the running costs of the company. This includes things like accountancy fees, postage, stationery, IT equipment and, controversially, training costs.

None of the above costs are deductible in calculating the Deemed Payment unless they relate directly to a relevant engagement and would have been deductible from employment income.

This brings us to expenses deductible in Step 3. There should not be many of these as usually it is quite hard for employees to claim expenses on a tax-free basis. However, it is much easier to claim travel and subsistence if you work through your own company.

If you can claim subsistence, then it is generally better to claim the HMRC approved benchmark rates, based on your daily hours, rather than actual costs where you would need to add up all the receipts. It usually works out better for you anyway.

You should be able to claim professional subscriptions if they are relevant to the work. You may also claim training costs, but only if they relate directly to the work and you were required to pass exams or attend courses in order to win the contract.

Capital allowances can only be claimed if you were *required* to use your own equipment. You cannot claim them if you use your own equipment out of choice, or for equipment not actually used in a relevant engagement during the year.

However, if you can claim capital allowances, then you can claim the whole cost of the relevant items up to the maximum Annual Investment Allowance, which is £250,000 from 1 January 2013.

Pension contributions are a useful deduction. If you are at risk of IR35, it is generally a good idea to make employer contributions rather than personal contributions so as to reduce your exposure.

Finally, you should apply the fraction 13.8 /113.8 to the running total at Step 7 in order to work out the employer's national insurance element.

IR35 Today

By 2011 it seemed that IR35 had become almost an irrelevance. HMRC had lost so many cases in the courts and tribunals that it appeared they had little appetite for enforcing it any longer.

In fact, only 322 IR35 investigations were opened by HMRC between April 2006 and March 2010, including just 23 in the 2010/11 tax year. It was said that you had more chance of winning the National Lottery than being investigated under IR35.

Then two things happened. First, the Office of Tax Simplification (OTS) released its long-awaited report into small business taxation in March 2011. Instead of recommending that IR35 be scrapped, as many had hoped and expected, its advice was to keep it on the statute books and improve the way it was administered.

Second, in February 2012, a political storm broke over revelations that thousands of top civil servants and BBC stars were being paid through their own companies and saving huge amounts of tax and national insurance. Suddenly, personal service companies were in the public eye as never before.

As a result, HMRC has had to up its game on IR35. In the wake of the OTS report, they set up an IR35 Forum with various interested groups with the aim of improving communication and agreeing better ways of administering the IR35 rules.

After consultations within the Forum, HMRC came up with their infamous Business Entity Tests. These are supposed to be a quick and easy way of telling which IR35 risk category your company falls into – high, medium, or low.

Technically, these tests are supposed to measure your risk of being *investigated* by HMRC, not whether you actually fall foul of IR35. That is just as well, as the tests are very generic and it is possible to be in the high-risk category even if you are clearly outside IR35. For example, many genuine firms are based at the owner's home, have no employees and charge daily/hourly rates. They would probably fail the key tests of premises, assistance and efficiency.

In fact, these tests have been heavily criticised for ignoring many factors already recognised by the courts as relevant to IR35 and even for ignoring commercial reality in some cases.

There are 12 tests with different points attached to each. By adding up the total points, you can assess which risk band you fall into:

Less than 10 points	High risk
10 to 20 points	Medium risk
More than 20 points	Low risk

If HMRC checks whether IR35 applies to you, and you can prove that you are in the low-risk band, they will generally close their IR35 enquiry, at least for the next three years.

The Business Entity Tests are as follows:

1. Business Premises Test. Does your business own or rent business premises which are separate both from your home and from the end client's premises? *Score 10 points if the answer is yes.*

2. PII Test. Do you need professional indemnity insurance? *Score 2 points if the answer is yes.*

3. Efficiency Test. Has your business had the opportunity in the last 24 months to increase its income by working more efficiently (e.g. contract clauses that pay you a fixed amount for a job even if you finish early)? *Score 10 points if the answer is yes.*

4. Assistance Test. Does your business engage any workers (other than the directors/shareholders) who bring in at least 25% of the yearly turnover? *Score 35 points if the answer is yes.*

5. Advertising Test. Has your business spent over £1,200 on advertising in the last 12 months? *Score 2 points if the answer is yes.*

6. Previous PAYE Test. Has the current client engaged you on PAYE employment terms within the 12 months that ended on the last 31 March, with no major changes to your working arrangements? *Score minus 15 points if answer is yes.*

7. Business Plan Test. Does your business have a business plan with a cash flow forecast that you update regularly? Does your business have a business bank account, identified as such by the bank, which is separate from your personal account? *Score 1 point if your answer to both questions is yes.*

8. Repair at Own Expense. Would your business have to bear the cost of having to put right any mistakes? *Score 4 points if your answer is yes.*

9. Client Risk Test. Has your business been unable to recover payment:
- For work done in the last 24 months
- More than 10% of yearly turnover?

Score 10 points if your answer is yes.

10. Billing Test. Do you invoice for work carried out before being paid and negotiate payment terms? *Score 2 points if your answer is yes.*

11. Right of Substitution Test. Does your business have the right to send a substitute? *Score 2 points if your answer is yes.*

12. Actual Substitution Test. Have you hired anyone in the last 24 months to do the work you have taken on? *Score 20 points if the answer is yes.*

These tests may provide a useful guide as to whether HMRC might want to investigate your tax affairs. However, the actual application of IR35 will always boil down to individual engagements and each contract must be looked at separately. Ultimately, professional advice will always be required to determine whether you are subject to IR35 or not.

If you receive a letter from HMRC asking if you have considered your IR35 status, my advice is to tell them why you believe IR35 does not apply to your contracts based on factors considered relevant by the **courts**, not the HMRC Business Entity Tests.

How to Avoid IR35

Now to the nitty gritty. If you are a contractor potentially affected by IR35, how do you go about avoiding it, or at least reducing your exposure? The following tips should be useful to you:

- **Get your contract reviewed.** There are many firms now specialising in IR35 contract reviews. They will identify the riskier clauses and give guidance on how to make your contract more resistant to IR35.

- **Get tax investigation insurance.** It costs very little to take out insurance covering you against the costs of an IR35 investigation, and is well worth it given the time, stress and expense of dealing with HMRC yourself.

- **Make your contract IR35 proof.** Not always possible if you work through an agency or have to sign a standard contract, but try to make sure it includes clauses that point away from employment and remove any that do.

166

- **Get your client on-side.** It always helps if the client is behind you and forewarned about IR35 issues. In particular, they should support any clauses you wish to rely on, such as your right to appoint a substitute.

- **Ensure your working arrangements reflect the contract.** If they don't, HMRC will simply ignore any clauses that do not reflect reality or are incapable of being exercised. So will the courts or tax tribunals if your case goes that far.

- **Get the client to sign a Confirmation of Working Arrangements.** This is a document setting out how your contract actually works in practice. It should reinforce any favourable clauses (such as substitution rights) that could be challenged by the taxman.

- **Self-assess your contract.** After a few weeks, set out in writing why you think the contract is outside the scope of IR35, making reference to your actual working arrangements, and email it to your accountant. This will show that you were reasonable and didn't just ignore IR35.

- **Operate as a business.** Set up a website, advertise for work, take out business insurance, do work for other clients, raise invoices for your fees, etc.

- **Do not keep too much money in your company.** If you do lose an IR35 investigation, only the cash in the company is at risk. Previous dividends should not be attacked so long as you were reasonable and did not deliberately flout IR35.

- **Pay company pension contributions.** If you are at risk of IR35, company pension contributions will reduce your exposure as these are deductible against tax and national insurance. Be sure not to exceed the tax-free limits though.

- **Avoid long-term contracts.** In general, the longer you work for one client the higher the risk of your contract falling foul of IR35. Stick to short-term contracts.

- **Don't become part of the furniture.** If you do have a long-term contract, try to avoid becoming part and parcel of the organisation. Don't get too involved in staff appraisals/recruitment, and don't appear on their website.

- **Make sure your work is project-based.** Projects are more indicative of self-employment. If your role covers routine work or is ongoing, that points more towards employment.

- **Try to work your own hours.** Freedom to come and go as you please would be a big plus in your favour if you can persuade the client to co-operate.

- **Appoint a substitute.** May be difficult, but if you can get the client to agree to this just for one day or a week whilst you are on holiday, that would defeat IR35 on its own. You would have to pay them yourself though.

- **Remedy defective work free of charge.** Often known as the "cock-up tactic" this would show that the clause in your contract is not just window-dressing. Best to warn the client first though if you wish to make use of this clause!

- **Don't take agency contracts at face value.** They often contain old clauses that suggest an employment relationship. Try to get these removed or modified if you can.

- **Be compliant.** Always make sure your PAYE and personal tax returns are filed on time with no errors. Late or erroneous returns may flag you up for investigation. Try to stay under their radar.

Lastly, if you are unfortunate enough to become embroiled in an IR35 investigation, do not allow yourself to become stressed at the tone of the correspondence from HMRC, or make statements that may come back to haunt you. Always follow the advice of your professional advisor.

HMRC are well known for trying to twist the facts in their favour in IR35 cases and misinterpret decisions from earlier cases. Do not let this gull you into feeling that your case is weaker than it really is. Be prepared for the long haul and stand your ground.

Office Holders

Originally the Government intended to beef up IR35 with new rules extending it to so-called "controlling persons". However, it was satisfied with the progress made in the public sector to curb off-payroll arrangements and extended it only to "office holders".

This is mainly intended to catch contractors filling public sector offices created by statute, who could previously have taken advantage of the exemption for office holders. They will now be caught by IR35 under both tax and national insurance legislation.

There were fears that it could be used to catch contractors filling interim directorships in the private sector too, but according to HMRC it is merely a tidying-up exercise. We must wait and see!

Public Opinion

You might also wish to consider the public opinion implications of using a personal service company. The issue of personal service companies became topical following revelations in the media about the head of the Student Loans Company being paid through one, along with thousands of other public sector staff.

However, it has to be said that the issue was not very well reported in the media, with practically no insight into how the tax system actually works. In particular, IR35 was hardly mentioned, despite being the taxman's main weapon against personal service companies.

A proper distinction should be drawn between aggressive and artificial tax avoidance schemes and ordinary tax-planning methods that have been used by small companies and individuals for many years. Most taxpayers do no more than utilise existing reliefs and allowances and time transactions to their best possible advantage.

Taking dividends rather than salary to avoid national insurance contributions is frowned on by some. However, one must also remember that if a limited company contractor takes more salary in preference to dividends, he/she becomes liable to both employee and employer national insurance contributions at a combined rate of up to 25.8%. Is that fair?

Part 7

Staff Share Schemes

Chapter 45

Introduction

Research in both the UK and the USA shows a strong link between employee share ownership and productivity. It has also been UK government policy over the last 30 years to encourage wider share ownership amongst both employees and the public at large.

Tax breaks have been an integral part of this policy. A number of employee schemes offering generous tax breaks have been introduced for both large and small companies.

Giving free or subsidised shares to employees is normally a taxable benefit that must be reported on their P11Ds. However, if it is an approved scheme, tax can be reduced or even avoided completely, as can the employer's national insurance contributions.

For most employers, it is well worth the time and trouble to use an approved scheme, despite the extra administration. The choice of scheme will depend upon the type and size of the company and its overall objectives.

There are four schemes approved by HM Revenue & Customs for employee share ownership.

- Share Incentive Plans
- Save As You Earn (SAYE) schemes
- Enterprise Management Incentives
- Company Share Option Plans

All have their own distinctive features and requirements. Likewise, the tax treatment varies from scheme to scheme.

There are also many unapproved staff share schemes that enjoy no tax breaks whatsoever but could be more attractive, being possibly more flexible and not subject to the rules and limitations of the approved schemes.

We will now look at the four approved schemes in more detail.

Chapter 46

Share Incentive Plans (SIPs)

Share Incentive Plans (SIPs) allow you to receive free shares from your employer without paying any tax or national insurance on them. If the shares rise in value while they're held inside the plan, the capital gains are also tax free.

There are four different types of shares you can own under a SIP:

- Free shares
- Partnership shares
- Matching shares
- Dividend shares

Free Shares

Employees can receive free shares worth up to £3,000 per tax year, based on their market value at that time.

Partnership Shares

You can also buy partnership shares tax free out of your salary (ie before income tax and national insurance is deducted).

The annual limit is £1,500 or 10% of your salary, whichever is less. However, your employer may exclude overtime or bonuses.

Matching Shares

If you buy partnership shares, you can also receive up to two free matching shares from your employer for each partnership share that you buy.

Not all employers offer matching shares – you need to check the plan rules. Those that do may not offer as many as two free shares.

For example, Vodafone allows employees to buy shares worth up to £125 per month (£1,500 per year) and provides one free matching share for each share bought by the employee.

Dividend Shares

If you receive dividends from your free, partnership or matching shares you can use them to buy more shares, which may then be re-invested in the plan, instead of taking the cash.

If you do this the dividends are tax free and do not need to be reported on your tax return.

Before 6th April 2013 there was a £1,500 annual limit on the total amount of dividend shares that could be re-invested in the SIP. This limit has now been removed but employers can still apply their own limits.

Qualifying Criteria

Your employer may link the award of free shares to certain criteria, including:

- Level of pay
- Length of service
- Hours worked
- Performance

The rules must be the same for everyone and all employees must be eligible to join the scheme at some point. Companies can require employees to have worked for a minimum period before qualifying but that period cannot be longer than 18 months.

In addition, part-time employees must be entitled to the same rights as full-time staff, subject to reasonable limits based on hours worked. A pro-rata entitlement based on your contracted working hours is the usual arrangement.

Performance can be the most problematic qualifying criterion as it has to be based on an objective measure that cannot be disputed. It can relate to individual employees, groups of employees or the company itself.

Time Limits

Free Shares

With free shares the minimum holding period is three years (from the date the shares are awarded) but can be up to five years if the company chooses.

You may forfeit your free shares if you leave the company before the minimum holding period is up. In this sense the shares may be seen as "golden handcuffs".

If you leave the company (or the group it belongs to) any shares that are not forfeited must be transferred to you. They will remain tax free if you leave early due to retirement, redundancy, injury or disability (the so-called "good leavers") but you may have tax and national insurance to pay if you leave for any other reason.

Partnership Shares

You can take partnership shares out of the plan at any time – after all, you will have paid for them yourself. However, you could lose any matching shares awarded with them if you remove them within three years.

Matching Shares

As with free shares, the minimum holding period is three years but can be up to five years if the company chooses. Otherwise, your employer may require you to forfeit them.

Dividend Shares

The minimum holding period is three years from the date of acquisition. Your employer cannot require you to forfeit dividend shares if you remove them before that, but you may lose tax relief.

After five years you can take your shares out of the plan without any tax implications whatsoever, apart from the fact that any increase in their value from that point onwards may be subject to capital gains tax.

Tax Treatment

Free Shares

If you keep your shares inside the plan for five years there will be no income tax or national insurance payable.

If you withdraw them any earlier you may face a tax bill.

Where shares are withdrawn from the plan within three years of being awarded, tax is payable, based on their market value on the date you remove them.

If you withdraw shares within three to five years, income tax is payable on the *lower* of the

- Market value when first awarded
- Market value on the date of withdrawal

National insurance is also payable when taking shares out of the plan early if they are "readily convertible assets". That would be the case if they are listed on a recognised stock exchange.

No income tax or national insurance is payable if you leave early due to injury, disability, redundancy or retirement, even though the shares must still be taken out of the plan.

If you die whilst the shares are still in the plan, they will pass to your estate and there will be no tax or national insurance to pay even if five years have not elapsed yet. However, your executors may have to pay capital gains tax when they sell them.

Partnership Shares

If the shares have been held for at least five years they can be removed from the plan without any income tax or national insurance being payable.

If partnership shares are withdrawn before they've been held for five years, income tax and national insurance may be payable:

- Where the shares have been held in the plan for less than three years, tax is payable on the market value of the shares at the time they are removed from the plan.

- Where the shares have been held for between three and five years, income tax is payable on the lesser of the salary used to buy the shares and the market value of the shares at the time they are removed from the plan.

You would also have to pay national insurance when taking shares out of the plan early if they are "readily convertible assets". That would be the case if they are listed on a recognised stock exchange.

Matching Shares

The tax treatment is the same as for free shares.

Dividend Shares

If dividends from plan shares are paid out in cash they are taxed in the usual way. Basic-rate taxpayers do not pay tax on their dividend income; higher-rate taxpayers pay tax at 25% on the cash dividend received. There is no national insurance on dividends.

Alternatively the dividends can be reinvested tax free in dividend shares.

Dividend shares must be held for three years. If the employee resigns during the holding period the dividend shares will be transferred out of the plan and income tax will payable on the original dividend amount.

After three years the dividend shares can be withdrawn tax free and if they are sold immediately there will be no capital gains tax.

Capital Gains Tax

No capital gains tax is payable when free shares, partnership shares and matching shares are either a) taken out of the plan or b) sold directly from the plan.

No capital gains tax will be payable on shares kept in the plan until you sell them, no matter how much they go up in value. However, you may have to pay tax on any increase in value between taking them out of the plan and selling them.

You will have no capital gains tax to pay if the gains do not exceed the annual CGT exemption (£10,900 in 2013/14) or if you have capital losses to offset against them. You can also deduct the selling costs from the gains, such as stockbroker fees.

If the shares actually lose value between exiting the plan and the disposal date, you can either use the loss against capital gains in the same year or carry it forward indefinitely to a later tax year.

Paying Income Tax on SIP Shares

If the shares are readily convertible to cash, your employer will normally deduct tax and national insurance on them from your salary. If you are a higher-rate taxpayer and your employer only deducts basic-rate tax, you will have to pay the extra tax later.

If the shares are **not** readily convertible to cash, your employer will not deduct income tax from your salary. Therefore, you will need to declare them on a tax return and pay the tax yourself by 31 January following the end of the tax year.

In that situation, you must inform HMRC by 5 October following the end of the tax year that you have tax to pay on the shares. They may then settle the liability by adjusting your tax code if the bill is less than £2,000.

Worked Example

We will now look at an example to see how much tax can be saved if you acquire shares through a share investment plan rather than an unapproved scheme. We shall assume that the employer is very generous and awards the maximum entitlement.

Tom works for XYZ plc and earns £51,500 per annum. He gets 300 XYZ shares a year as part of his remuneration package and the shares are quoted at £10. Tom also wishes to buy 150 XYZ shares and his employer will then give him 300 matching XYZ shares.

XYZ pays a dividend of £2 per share and Tom intends to invest the dividends in more XYZ shares rather than take them in cash.

How much net income will Tom have after tax, national insurance and the cost of the shares?

	Approved Scheme	Unapproved Scheme
Annual salary	£51,500	£51,500
600 free/matching shares	0	£6,000
150 partnership shares	- £1,500	0
Taxable income	£50,000	£57,500
Income tax at 20%	£6,402	£6,402
Income tax at 40%	£3,420	£6,420
Employee NI at 12%	£4,044	£4,044
Employee NI at 2%	£171	£321
Total tax and NI	£14,037	£17,187
Annual salary	£51,500	£51,500
Total tax and NI	- £14,037	- £17,187
Net pay received	£37,463	£34,313
Cost of the shares	- £1,500	- £1,500
Tax on dividend	0	- £375
Net income	£35,963	£32,438

Based on 2013/14 tax/NI rates and allowances

We can see from the above example that Tom will end up with an extra £3,525 of net income in an approved share scheme.

If Tom has children, he will save even more money as he can avoid the new child benefit tax charge with an approved share scheme. Let's suppose he has three children under the age of 16 and his wife is entitled to child benefit of £2,449 a year.

With the approved scheme, Tom can reduce his "adjusted net income" to £50,000 by buying the partnership shares, so avoiding any tax on the child benefit.

With the unapproved scheme, his 'adjusted net income' rises to £57,500 and tax on the child benefit would be £1,836.

For employees earning over £100,000 or £150,000 there would be similar dire effects as a result of losing some or all of their personal allowance or moving into the 45% tax bracket.

Finally, there is capital gains tax to consider. If Tom keeps his XYZ shares in the plan for five years before selling them for £18 per share, he would be outside the scope of capital gains tax altogether.

However, with an unapproved scheme, there would be a capital gain of £6,000 to go on his tax return (potentially).

As the annual exemption for capital gains tax is currently £10,900 the whole gain could be sheltered and no CGT would be payable. However, if Tom had other gains using up his annual exemption for that year, he would be taxed on the full £6,000 at 28%.

That would cost him £1,680 in capital gains tax.

In total, therefore, Tom could save up to £7,041 per year with an approved share investment plan, calculated as follows:

Income tax and national insurance	£3,525
Tax on child benefit (for 3 children)	£1,836
Capital gains tax (if no exemption)	£1,680
Total	**£7,041**

Employers are also better off with an approved scheme, since they will avoid class 1 national insurance at 13.8% on the free/matching shares. They will also avoid it on the partnership shares as these reduce taxable pay.

In the above example, the employer would save £1,035.

Chapter 47

Save As You Earn (SAYE)
Share Options

Save As You Earn (SAYE) share option schemes promote widespread employee share ownership as the scheme must be available to all qualifying employees. They also nurture staff loyalty as the options must be held for at least three years.

How SAYE Schemes Work

Unlike with Share Investment Plans, employers do not simply give away free shares. Instead, they grant you an *option* to buy shares at an agreed price after three or five years. Meanwhile, you have to save a fixed monthly sum in a bank or building society account.

You can't use just any old bank account, like your existing savings account. It must be a special certified SAYE savings arrangement operated by an HMRC-approved financial institution. A SAYE Sharesave scheme is the usual choice.

The account will then be linked to the employer's SAYE scheme.

You can save any amount from £5 to £250 a month over a three-year or five-year period. Once the monthly sum has been fixed it cannot be changed. You are stuck with it until the three-year or five-year period is up (unless you decide to cancel the SAYE scheme altogether).

All employees over the age of 16 may qualify for SAYE options. However, an employer can impose a minimum qualification period of up to five years' service, so not all staff may be able to participate immediately.

Bear in mind that you may not necessarily be allowed to pay in the maximum £250. Your employer can reduce this if he wishes or have different limits for different groups of staff. Often these are linked to level of pay or length of service.

Exercising SAYE Options

SAYE options normally become exercisable on the 'bonus date' – the date when repayment of your contributions falls due. You then get six months to exercise your options.

SAYE options cannot normally be exercised for at least three years from the date they are granted. The main exceptions are:

- **Good Leavers**. Where employees leave the company due to redundancy, retirement, injury or disability during the option period. I would stress that the word "good" has a special meaning here.

- **Death**. Where employees die whilst still employed by the company during the option period.

- **Change of Control**. Where a third party acquires the whole of the ordinary share capital under the terms of an offer where control of the company is a condition.

There are a few other circumstances, such as an amalgamation, company reconstruction or voluntary winding-up, where it is permissible for SAYE options to be exercised within three years.

Only in the case of good leavers and death is it compulsory for the employer to allow options to be exercised. In the other circumstances, options can only be exercised within three years if the scheme rules permit it.

If you are on sabbatical or on secondment you can now keep your SAYE options. The same goes for those on long-term sick leave, maternity leave, parental or adoption leave, and for reservists called up for military service.

In all these cases, it must be anticipated that the employee will return to work, otherwise the normal leaving rules will apply. If an employee leaves the company for any other reason before the first three years are up, the SAYE options must lapse.

In the case of five-year plans, if you leave between three and five years the options will only lapse if the scheme rules require it.

Tax Implications

The tax savings from SAYE share options come in three ways:

Firstly, you will be exercising the options at a price agreed with HMRC when the options were originally granted, which will normally be based on the market value of the shares at that date (if quoted on a recognised stock exchange).

You would hope that after three years or five years the shares would be worth a lot more (although Northern Rock staff were famously disappointed). Happy days if they are, as any increase in the share price during the option period will be totally tax free.

Secondly, the option price set by the employer can be as low as 80% of market value on the date they were granted. So even if the share price does not go up, you can still get a discount of up to 20% tax free.

The third tax-saving opportunity is sadly not available at present as interest rates are so low. You used to get a tax-free bonus at the end of the option period in lieu of interest. The bonus rates are set each year and based on a multiple of your monthly contributions.

Unfortunately, the bonus rates are zero at present. So is the interest rate on early repayments. The only good news is that the bonus rate is set at the time the option is granted, so older schemes may still pay bonuses.

Current and previous SAYE bonus rates can be found on the following page of the HMRC website:

www.hmrc.gov.uk/shareschemes/historical-bonus-rates.pdf

There is no income tax charge on the exercise of the options, no matter how much the shares may have risen in value, provided you keep them in the plan for the minimum three or five years.

Gains used to be taxed when options were exercised early due to a change in control of the company. A recent change (July 2013) means that these gains will now be exempt if the acquiring company pays you cash and there was no opportunity to exchange your options for new ones.

Worked Example

We will now see how much tax you can potentially save with SAYE share options. As the tax savings are based mainly on how much the share price goes up during the option period, they could in theory be limitless.

This example assumes average growth in the share price of 5% per annum. It also assumes the employer is very generous and allows the maximum £250 per month, plus the maximum 20% discount on the price of the shares.

ABC plc granted Alison a five-year SAYE option in October 2008 at a price of £2 per share. At that time the bonus for five-year schemes was seven monthly payments. Therefore, her total repayment under the plan will be £250 x 67 months = £16,750.

The option allows her to buy exactly 8,375 shares in ABC plc in October 2013 at £2 each.

The shares were quoted at £2.50 in October 2008. After five years they have gone up to £3.20. On exercising the option, she will be able to make an immediate profit as follows:

Sale proceeds (8,375 x £3.20)	£26,800
Acquisition cost (8,375 x £2.00)	£16,750
Increase in value	£10,050

This profit is tax free under an approved SAYE scheme. If the scheme was not approved, she would have to pay income tax at her top rate of tax on the increase in value. Assuming she is a higher-rate taxpayer, 40% tax would have come to £4,020.

She might also have to pay extra tax if she breaches other key income thresholds: £50,000 for child benefit, £100,000 for the personal allowance restriction and £150,000 for 45% tax.

If she subsequently sells the shares for more than £2 each she will make a capital gain and potentially incur capital gains tax at 18% or 28%. However, she would have to do this anyway, whether the scheme is approved or unapproved, so capital gains tax is neutral.

In any case, her gain may well be fully covered by her annual capital gains tax exemption (£10,900 in 2013/14).

Chapter 48

Enterprise Management Incentives

If the objective is to recruit or retain key staff, small companies are better off giving their employees share options under an Enterprise Management Incentive (EMI) scheme. These allow the employees to benefit from a future sale or flotation of the company.

Employers can pick and choose who they offer these to. They do not have to be made available to all staff. As an added incentive the award can also be linked to predetermined performance measures, such as sales targets.

Employers can impose other conditions too, such as requiring the options to lapse if the employee leaves.

EMI options are ideal for small companies that are growing fast and expect to be bought out by a larger competitor or float on the stock market one day. As the options do not have to be exercised for 10 years, they are suitable for long-term planning.

Your employer will offer you EMI options for a certain number of shares at a predetermined price. In order to get tax relief these options can be held for a maximum of 10 years before they must be exercised. The options themselves are not taxable.

Once the options are exercised (usually when the company is bought out or floated on the stock exchange) a tax charge will arise on the difference between the option price and the value of the shares at the date granted (or exercised if this is lower).

If the company was not quoted on a recognised stock exchange on the date the options are granted, the company will have had to agree a value for its shares with HMRC. It is this value that will be used when the options are eventually exercised.

If the company granted you the options free, then you will be taxed on the full value of the shares at the date of grant. If you have to pay for the shares (at the option price) only the discount to the market value at the date of grant (if any) will be taxed.

Obviously you would expect the shares to go up in value substantially over 10 years, especially if the company does well. In that case, the entire gain will be tax free. The company will deduct the option price plus any tax due and pay you the net proceeds.

Qualifying Criteria

EMI schemes must satisfy many criteria in order to qualify for the advantageous tax treatment. These relate to the company granting the options, the individual employees and the scheme.

The Company

Only companies with gross assets of up to £30 million qualify for the EMI scheme and they must have fewer than the *equivalent* of 250 full-time employees when the options are granted. Part-time employees count pro-rata based on 35 full-time hours per week.

Also, they must be carrying on a qualifying trading activity as defined by the tax rules for the EMI scheme. There are some surprising exclusions here. For example, ship-building, banking, farming, running a hotel and legal services are all excluded.

The company in whose shares the options are granted must be independent. It must not be controlled by another company (i.e. it must not be a subsidiary of a group company).

The Employee

To qualify for EMI options, you must be an employee or director of the company in whose shares the options are to be granted, or any qualifying subsidiary of that company. Therefore, you are allowed options in the shares of a parent company.

You must also work at least 25 hours a week for that company or, if less, at least 75% of your working time. This is based on average working time. You must continue to satisfy this requirement after the option is granted or it will be a disqualifying event.

The 75% limit is based on total *remunerative* time including other jobs and self-employment. Whether you actually do any work or not is immaterial. You merely need to be paid for it. This includes self-employed work undertaken with a view to profit. In theory, you could get away with just one hour a week if you do no other work. However, if you have another job or business that takes up say five hours per week, you must work at least 16 hours per week for the company in whose shares the option is granted in order to meet the 75% requirement.

In calculating your total working time, you can count sick leave, holidays, pregnancy, maternity or paternity leave, parental leave and any notice period you are not required to work upon the termination of your employment.

No employee or director can hold EMI options worth more than £250,000 at any one time (based on their value at the time they were granted). Any options in excess of this will be disqualified. Up to 15 June 2012 the individual limit was just £120,000.

Once an employee has reached the £250,000 limit, no further EMI options can be granted for at least three years and only then if some options have been exercised so they are now below the £250,000.

There is also a material interest test of 30%. This means that no employee (either alone or together with his associates) can control more than 30% of the ordinary share capital of the company.

If the employee only acquires a material interest greater than 30% after an option has been granted, it will not be a disqualifying event but he/she will not be eligible for any more EMI options until his/her material interest has been reduced to 30% or less.

The material interest test does not include shares that are still under EMI options but does include CSOP options. If these will be newly issued shares when the options are exercised, they must be added to the current shares for the purpose of assessing the 30%.

The Scheme

The unrestricted market value of all EMI options granted by a company (as at the date of grant) must never exceed £3 million. Otherwise, the option that causes the £3 million limit to be breached will not qualify for tax relief.

The share options must be capable of being exercised within 10 years in order to get tax relief. Otherwise the employee will be taxed on the difference between the option price and the market value of the shares on the date the option was exercised.

The option must be granted for the commercial purpose of recruiting or retaining an employee. It must not be part of a scheme of arrangement, the main purpose of which is to avoid tax.

The employer must notify HM Revenue & Customs of the award of each option granted under the scheme within 92 days and file an annual return within three months of the end of each tax year.

There must be a written agreement between the company and the employee confirming, amongst other things, the date the option was granted, the exercise price of the option and how/when the option may be exercised.

The employee must confirm in writing that he/she satisfies the working time requirement at the date the option was granted.

The shares to which the EMI option relates must form part of the ordinary share capital of the company and be non-redeemable.

The option must be exercised within 90 days of a disqualifying event, such as a takeover or merger, in order to qualify for full tax relief. The previous limit was 40 days but this was changed with effect from 17 July 2013.

In the event of a company takeover, the options may be replaced by options for shares in the acquiring company within six months of the takeover, provided they satisfy certain conditions and are capable of being exercised by the original 10-year deadline.

Tax Implications

As already mentioned, you only pay tax on the exercise of an EMI share option if the price is less than the agreed market value of the shares on the date the option was granted (or the current market value if this happens to be lower).

If there is a tax liability, the employer must deduct both tax and national insurance contributions from the sale proceeds if the shares are "readily convertible assets". That will be the case if they are listed on a recognised stock exchange or trading arrangements are already in place (or soon will be) when the shares are acquired.

If the shares are not readily convertible assets, there will be no national insurance to pay and the employee must pay any tax liability directly to HMRC by 31 January following the end of the tax year in which the option is exercised.

The employer may, under the terms of the EMI scheme, require the employee to pay any national insurance contributions they incur. Hence, you may end up paying both employee and employer national insurance contributions.

If an EMI option is not exercised within 90 days of a disqualifying event, there may be extra tax and national insurance to pay. This will be based on the increase in market value between the date of exercise and immediately before the disqualifying event.

If the disqualifying event was the employee failing to meet the working time requirement, it will be deemed to have occurred at the end of that particular tax year.

If the shares are not sold immediately when an EMI option is exercised, there may be capital gains tax to pay on any increase in value between the exercise date and the eventual disposal date. This must be paid by 31 January following the end of the tax year.

As from 6 April 2013, Entrepreneurs Relief will be granted on the disposal of any shares acquired through an EMI scheme, even if the normal conditions for this relief, such as 12 months' ownership and a minimum 5% shareholding, are not satisfied.

This is a very generous additional tax relief as it reduces the capital gains tax rate from a possible 28% to just 10%. In addition, you can claim your annual CGT exemption (currently £10,900) against any gains on the shares.

Worked Example

We will now study a theoretical example to see how much tax you could save by taking share options through an approved EMI scheme rather than an unapproved scheme.

This example assumes that the employee is awarded the maximum amount each year under an EMI scheme and that the market value of the shares increases by 10% per annum. There is no discount given on the option price to market value.

Joe has worked as sales manager for CDE Ltd since 1 January 2004. He was granted an option when he joined and then on each anniversary for the next nine years with a view to awarding him the maximum possible number of shares under the EMI rules.

The final option in 2013 was calculated to bring his total holding up to the new limit of £250,000. On 31 March 2013 CDE Ltd was bought out at £30 per share and Joe exercised all his options within 40 days of the takeover.

Option Date	Share Value	No of Shares	Option Prices	Exercise Values	Gain on Exercise
1 Jan 04	£12.00	1,000	£12,000	£30,000	£18,000
1 Jan 05	£13.20	909	£11,999	£27,270	£15,271
1 Jan 06	£14.52	826	£11,994	£24,780	£12,786
1 Jan 07	£15.97	751	£11,993	£22,530	£10,537
1 Jan 08	£17.57	683	£12,000	£20,490	£8,490
1 Jan 09	£19.33	620	£11,985	£18,600	£6,615
1 Jan 10	£21.26	565	£12,012	£16,950	£4,938
1 Jan 11	£23.38	513	£11,994	£15,390	£3,396
1 Jan 12	£25.72	466	£11,985	£13,980	£1,995
1 Jan 13	£28.30	5,019	£142,038	£150,570	£8,532
Totals			**£250,000**	**£340,560**	**£90,560**

Now if Joe had acquired all these options through an approved EMI scheme, there would be no tax whatsoever on the total gain as the option prices are not less than the market value at the date of grant. The increase in their value would be entirely tax free.

However, if the scheme was unapproved and Joe was earning say £80,000 a year, he would pay tax on the gain at a top rate of 45% plus 2% national insurance. He would also lose his personal allowance as his income for the year would exceed £100,000.

His tax and national insurance liability would increase by £42,839 altogether. That is a marginal rate of 47.3% on the total gain.

If CDE Ltd had not been bought out, Joe would have had to exercise the 2004 option by 31 December 2013. If the share price then was £31, for example, the gain would have been £19,000.

With an unapproved scheme, his total income for 2013/14 would have been £99,000 (again assuming a salary of £80,000) which is just below the £100,000 threshold. Therefore, he would not have lost any of his personal allowance. His tax and national insurance liability that year would have gone up by £7,980 – a mere 42%.

This is a rather extreme example as not many employers award their staff the maximum EMI limit. Also, not many shares go up 150% in 10 years. However, it does illustrate the potential tax savings with EMI options.

Chapter 49

Company Share Option Plans

These are discretionary schemes that can be used by any employer regardless of size or trade. Hence, if your employer does not qualify for EMI options, it could offer you a CSOP instead. However, it is not mandatory to make them available to all staff.

CSOPs are traditionally offered by large employers, not qualifying for the EMI scheme, as a perk to their senior executives. However, there is a limit of £30,000 on the total value you can hold at any one time, and this has been frozen since 1996.

Consequently, their popularity as executive share options has declined somewhat. £30,000 is not much of an incentive these days to top bankers and other executives looking for a competitive remuneration package.

As with EMI schemes, the employer gives you an option to buy its shares at some time in the future at a predetermined price. If the share price is higher when you exercise the option, you will not be taxed on the difference.

However, there could be capital gains tax to pay on any increase in the value of the shares after you exercise the option. This may well be the case if you decide to hold them as an investment or if there happens to be no market yet for the shares.

In that event, they will not qualify for Entrepreneurs Relief unless you hold the shares for a year and own more than 5% of the ordinary share capital. That is very unlikely for a public company although it might well be the case for a small private company.

Like EMI, there is a maximum period of 10 years between the date of grant and the date of exercise. Any CSOP options not exercised within 10 years will lapse. However, there is also a three-year minimum period during which the options cannot be exercised.

It is worth noting that employers no longer need to specify a retirement age in a CSOP scheme, as this would breach new laws on age discrimination and compulsory retirement.

Differences with EMI

As CSOPs are share option plans there are many similarities to EMI schemes but also some important differences you need to be aware of. The key ones are as follows:

	CSOP	EMI
Maximum value	£30,000	£250,000
Option period	3-10 years	0-10 years
Option price	At least market value	No minimum
Working time	No minimum	25 hours or 75%
Directors	Full time only	Subject to above
Material interest *	Over 25%	Over 30%
Disqualifying events	No tax relief	90 days to exercise
Tax-free early exercise	Good leavers only	As per scheme rules

*As from 17 July 2013 the material interest limit for **new** CSOP options was raised to 30% to align them with the EMI rules.*

How CSOPs Work

To be awarded CSOP options, the only requirement is that you must be an employee of the company granting the options (or of a constituent company in a group scheme). Consultancy work on a self-employed basis or via your own company does not count.

There is no statutory working time requirement for employees as there is with EMI schemes, although directors must be full-time. Part-time directors do not qualify.

For this purpose, 25 hours per week is normally sufficient for a director to qualify as full-time. However, any hours worked as a consultant do not count, only those as a director. In addition, he/she must be on the payroll for those hours and subject to PAYE.

Employers can still specify a minimum number of working hours themselves in the scheme rules if they wish, so part-time staff may still be excluded. CSOP schemes are discretionary anyway, so in practice employers can choose whom they offer them to.

The main difference with EMI schemes (apart from the much lower maximum value) is that the options must normally be held for at least three years in order to qualify for tax relief.

There is no legal necessity for the options to lapse if you cease being an employee, even if you leave within the first three years before the options can be exercised (although you would normally then lose the tax relief if the option had to be exercised immediately).

Only "good leavers" are allowed to exercise their options tax-free within the first three years, provided they do so within six months. There are four ways of being a good leaver – injury, disability, retirement, and redundancy. Illness does not count.

However, even "good leavers" are only allowed to exercise their options early if the scheme rules permit it. There is no automatic right to do so. The law merely allows them to get tax relief on options exercised within three years if the scheme allows it.

In fact, employers can insist on leavers losing their options altogether if they wish. They can also specify a minimum length of service for the options to remain valid or insist that the shares are sold immediately (known as pre-emption provisions).

If you die before the first three years are up, the options may be exercised by your personal representatives within 12 months of your death (if the scheme rules permit it) without a tax charge arising. This is the only way your options can ever be transferred.

From 17 July 2013, you can also exercise CSOP options within three years without a tax charge arising if it was due to a takeover or a business transfer subject to TUPE regulations, but they must be exercised within six months of the relevant event taking place.

This is a sensible revision to the rules as obviously it is beyond your control if your company is taken over. Unfortunately, it does not necessarily apply to CSOP options granted before this date. It depends on the scheme rules when they were granted.

Another key difference with EMI schemes is that CSOP options must be priced at their market value (as at the date of grant). Employers are not allowed to award options free or discounted shares under the scheme. However, any increase in market value that occurs after the options are granted is fine. This will be tax free, and it will also not count towards the £30,000 limit for the grant of future options as this is always based on their value at the date of grant.

For example, if you have an option to buy 1,000 shares at £10 each (their value at the time) that leaves you £20,000 for future options. If market value goes up to £20 you can have an option for another 1,000 shares at £20 each as the first 1,000 are not re-valued.

For this reason, a company should always agree a market value for its shares with HMRC before any options are granted, unless they are quoted on a recognised stock exchange, in which case there are specific provisions for determining their value.

It is possible for CSOP options to be made conditional on the attainment of targets by either the employee/division (e.g. sales) or the company (e.g. profits, turnover). This is permissible provided the targets are capable of objective measurement.

You can also have parallel options, whereby one automatically lapses if or when the other is exercised. This enables employers to allow different numbers of shares to be bought, and/or at different prices, according to whether or not targets have been met.

Worked Example

Harry works for EFG plc and on 1 June 2003 was granted a 10-year option for 10,000 shares at £3.00 each, which was the market value at the time. The shares go up 5% per annum and on 1 April 2013 the company was bought for £4.65 per share.

If the option was unapproved he would be taxed on the difference of £1.65 per share x 10,000 = £16,500. As a higher-rate taxpayer he would pay 40% tax plus 2% employee national insurance, so total deductions would be £6,930.

The net proceeds would be £9,570 after paying the option price of £30,000. However, if it was an approved CSOP option, he would pay no tax or national insurance at all on its exercise and take home the full gain of £16,500.

Part 8

Running a Part-time Business

Chapter 50

Part-time Businesses: How They Are Taxed

Many people hold down a full-time job but also have a part-time business that earns them a bit of extra money (for example selling things on eBay, doing DIY jobs etc, running evening classes, etc).

How do you pay tax on this income or, more to the point, how can you minimise the tax payable or even avoid it altogether? After all, not all money that you receive from other people is taxable. For instance, petrol money is not normally taxable.

It all depends on your motivation for doing the work in the first place. To be taxed as trading profits, there has to be a trade. Just because you sell something or do some work for someone, that does not mean there is a trade.

Whether you are trading or not can be a very grey area as there is no statutory definition of trading. However, there is a wealth of case law on the subject, which is often relied on by the taxman to decide whether you should be taxed as a trader or not.

The Badges of Trade

Over the years, the courts have come to recognise certain patterns of behaviour as having the characteristics of a trade. These are known as the "Badges of Trade" and include:

- Whether there was a trading motive
- The frequency of the transactions
- The type of asset involved
- The quantity of assets bought and sold
- Whether or not there is an existing trade
- Whether the asset has been modified or adapted
- The financial arrangements for buying and selling
- The length of time the assets are held before selling
- How exactly the asset was sold
- How the asset was acquired in the first place

Are You an Employee?

If you are an employee then your employer is legally obliged to operate PAYE on your earnings and pay any income tax and national insurance to HMRC. However, if you are self-employed, it is your responsibility to register with HMRC, complete a tax return once a year and pay income tax and national insurance. But how do you know whether you are employed or self-employed?

Usually the answer is obvious. You are taken on as an employee, given a contract of employment and receive a payslip showing tax and national insurance deducted from your earnings. However, sometimes it is less clear-cut, especially for casual services.

The firm or person you are working for may not want you all the time. It might be just a part-time, casual or one-off arrangement, or maybe they hire you for your expert knowledge and just leave you to get on with the job without any supervision.

The distinction between employment and self-employment then becomes blurred. It may not be obvious to either party. This is more important for the business paying you because if they get it wrong, they will be clobbered with the tax bill, not you.

The following factors are usually relevant in deciding whether you are an employee or not:

- Whether you work for anyone else or just this firm/person
- Who controls the work (i.e. how, when or where it is done)
- Whether the work is a single task or a range of related tasks
- Whether the work is ongoing or ends on completion of a task
- Whether you operate as a genuine business for that work
- Whether you can sub-contract or delegate the work to others
- Use of your own equipment or software to do the work
- The basis on which you are paid (i.e. fixed fee, hourly rate, etc)
- The opportunity to make a profit or the risk of making a loss
- Whether you have to remedy any defects at your own cost
- Whether you guarantee your work or offer any refunds
- How you are paid (i.e. time-sheets, invoices, wage slips)
- The length of time you work for that particular firm/person

As you can see, it is a pretty grey area!

Miscellaneous Income

It is possible that you may be neither employed nor self-employed. Take someone who does odd jobs for friends or neighbours. He is not their employee and if these are just casual jobs, on the spur of the moment, with no plans to make it a permanent business, he is not trading either. His main aim is to help his friends and neighbours. He does not, therefore, need to register with the taxman as self-employed.

That is not to say he owes no tax on the money, however. All income derived from work is subject to income tax and must be declared on the Miscellaneous Income page of your tax return, net of any expenses incurred doing it.

The same goes for other types of miscellaneous income such as royalties or one-off fees. For example, you may write magazine articles or supply photographs occasionally. It is not trading but you still have to declare the income on your tax return.

Cashbacks, however, are exempt. The taxman accepts that these are effectively rebates on your spending rather than income, so no need to declare the cashbacks from your credit card or loyalty cards, or from cashback websites such as Quidco.com.

Reimbursed Expenses

Sometimes people may pay you money to cover your expenses so you don't end up out of pocket. Petrol money is a good example. You give someone a lift and they offer to pay for some of the fuel.

Even if the cash is more than sufficient to cover the cost you don't need to declare it. As long as you don't deliberately set out to make money as a *de facto* taxi driver, you will be OK.

The same goes for domestic arrangements where someone gives you money towards household bills, a restaurant bill or the cost of a holiday. Anything in excess of the costs you incur would be regarded as gratuitous (a gift) and not, therefore, taxable.

However, if you incur those expenses in the course of a **business**, then any cash you receive towards those expenses should be taxed as part of your trading profits.

Selling Possessions

Many people sell old possessions they no longer want on eBay (and similar websites) or at car boot sales, allowing them to reduce clutter around the house and earn a little cash into the bargain.

Is this sort of activity taxable? The answer is no in most cases. Only if your selling turns into trading would you become liable to income tax and class 4 national insurance. Once you start buying second-hand goods and selling them for a profit, that's when you cross the line and become a trader.

As long as you stick to old possessions you want to get rid of, you should be OK. That may be more difficult than you think. Selling old stuff on eBay can quickly become compulsive!

The taxman trawls sites like eBay looking for secret traders all the time. They even have special software for it, so if you advertise items for sale regularly online, don't be surprised if you get a letter from HMRC.

Capital Gains Tax

Although you may not be subject to income tax when you sell your possessions, capital gains tax might bite if you sell something for more than £6,000.

Most personal possessions are regarded as *chattels* and there is no capital gains tax if you sell them for less than £6,000. Even then there may not be anything to pay because of the way the tax is worked out. That £6,000 limit has been frozen for decades now though, so it's not worth anything like as much as it used to be.

Capital gains tax may particularly affect people selling antiques. On shows like *Cash in the Attic* or *Antiques Roadshow* you often see some dusty old family heirloom that was previously used as a doorstop turn out to be worth several thousand pounds. There may well be capital gains tax to pay on such items.

You get an annual allowance for capital gains tax though and for 2013/14 this is £10,900. That should be enough to cover any gains you make on such items, assuming you haven't used up your allowance already.

Cars

How about cars? After all, they count as chattels and they often sell second-hand for a lot more than £6,000. Is there capital gains tax to pay? You will be pleased to hear that cars are exempt, even classic ones that actually appreciate in value.

This stands to reason really, because cars usually sell for a lot less than you pay for them. If they were not exempt from capital gains tax, car owners would have huge capital losses that could be offset against taxable capital gains from other assets.

There is no exemption from income tax if you are a motor dealer though, and, as we have seen, there can be a thin line between trading and selling old possessions. If you are in the habit of changing cars very frequently, you could be accused of dealing.

That may not be the case if you use the car as your own private vehicle for a short period and only sell one at a time. Plenty of people do make a living selling cars from the street, however, and tax is the last thing they think about until HMRC comes knocking. They could end up with a VAT bill too.

However, it is always your intention that counts, so if you can convince the taxman that you just get bored with cars very quickly, and you weren't looking for a fast profit, you might get away with it. On the other hand, maybe you won't!

Property Developers

If you are left a house by a dearly departed relative, and you decide to do it up before selling, are your profits taxable? Yes and No. You won't pay income tax or national insurance as it was not acquired with a view to trading, but there may well be capital gains tax.

That is not so bad, as the top rate of CGT is 28% and there's the annual CGT exemption too, whereas income tax and national insurance could be anything up to 47%. By and large, therefore, you would want the sale of your house to fall into the capital gains tax regime.

Furthermore, your renovation costs are deductible in working out your taxable gain, as are your buying and selling costs.

For habitual property developers, however, capital gains tax is very unlikely to be an option. Unless you can persuade the taxman that you bought the house as an investment or as somewhere to live, they will regard it as trading. That means paying income tax.

Sometimes the line can be very thin indeed. For instance, if you have no other properties in your name and actually live in the house after renovating it, you could claim that you bought it as your future residence instead.

That is the ideal scenario, for it means that not only do you avoid income tax and national insurance on any profit you make from selling the house, you can also avoid capital gains tax, as you will be entitled to private residence relief on the whole gain.

It would be wise not to do that too often though, as repeated gains from properties that you only live in for a short while may end up being taxable. You must intend the house to be a "residence" for at least the foreseeable future, even if it is not your only home.

In the worst-case scenario, you could end up paying income tax as it might be argued that you bought the house with the express intention of selling it for a profit after renovating it. The fact that you lived there for a short while would make no difference.

The taxman is usually quite sensible about this, as most people hope and expect to sell a house for more than they paid for it. Only if selling at a profit was your **main** motivation for buying the house in the first place will you be considered to be trading.

You sometimes see people on programmes like *Property Ladder* or *Homes under the Hammer* talking about selling a house once they have done it up. If the taxman is watching they will be treated as property developers, as their clear intention is to make a profit.

You can also avoid being treated as a trader if you buy a house for its investment potential. That may seem to be the same thing, but investment is more long-term. If you buy a house with the intention of letting it out, that will then fall into the CGT regime.

So what can you do to avoid being taxed as a property developer? Firstly, you will not be classified as one if you inherited the house. However, if you bought the house with half an eye on selling it, you should either live there yourself for a while or let it out.

How long you must live there or let it out is an unknown quantity. It will depend on various factors, but if it turns out to be for a very short time, things like sending your kids to school in the local area or being on the electoral register will help you argue your case.

Loss Relief

So far we've talked about the taxation of profits from part-time businesses and miscellaneous income, but what about losses? How are they treated for tax purposes?

The answer is very generously. For starters, you are allowed to offset any losses against **all** your other income in that tax year, so you could get a rebate for tax deducted under PAYE. You could also carry it back against profits for the previous year.

Failing that, you can also carry it forward against any future profits from the same business – indefinitely. You do have to tell HMRC about losses within four years otherwise you lose them, but as you would be self-employed you would be filling out an annual tax return anyway.

The cherry on the cake comes if you make losses in the first four years of starting a business, or in the last year before you end it. In both cases, you can offset losses against all your income up to three years before. This carry-back facility is very useful indeed, especially if your business has a lot of up-front expenditure.

You need to be careful about how you compute your loss though. It has to be based on proper accounting principles, with due allowance made for accruals, prepayments, debtors, creditors, personal drawings and stock.

Whatever you do, don't elect for the new cash accounting scheme that came into force in April 2013 if you make a loss, as it does not allow you to claim losses against your other income at all. All you can do is carry them forward against future profits.

Incidentally, this also applies to landlords and furnished holiday lets. You are not allowed to claim losses from property against your other income (unless it arises from capital allowances) although you can usually offset a loss on one property against a profit on another.

You should also bear in mind that trading losses were capped with effect from 6 April 2013. You can now only claim losses of up to £50,000 or 25% of your income, whichever is greater.

This rule was brought in to stop wealthy individuals reducing their tax bills to practically zero. If the average person made a loss of £50,000 he would have a lot more to worry about than tax relief!

There is also a rule capping your losses at £25,000 unless you work at least 10 hours a week in your business. This rule was brought in to stop "sleeping partners" claiming huge losses.

However, both these rules only apply to losses relieved against your **other** income in the same tax year or previous tax years. It does not affect losses carried forward against future profits from the same business.

Losses from Hobbies

Hobbies are usually things that *cost* you money. You would not normally expect to make a profit from your hobby, and even if you did, it would soon be classified as trading instead. For this reason, HMRC does not normally allow you to claim losses from hobbies.

However, sometimes you can combine a hobby with a business, and if you genuinely and reasonably *intend* to make a profit from it in the long run, then you can register it as a business and claim any losses that you may incur.

The key words here are *genuinely* and *reasonably*. Not many people expect to make money out of their hobbies, and even if they did set out hoping to make a profit, it must have been reasonable for them to do so otherwise any losses will be disallowable.

The distinction here can be hard to make in practice. Let me give you two examples, fictional of course:

Caroline is very artistic and enjoys putting photographic images of flowers on canvas. She displays her handiwork on her website and in art galleries. Her website allows customers to place orders and they can also order from the art galleries.

There is a very definite intention to make a profit here and quite correctly she registers as self-employed and completes a tax return. Unfortunately the business does not take off. The website does not get much traffic and an exhibition at the art gallery was cancelled.

As a result she makes a loss. Her costs (materials, website hosting, insurance, advertising, bank charges and use of home as office) outweigh revenue from the few sales she made. This loss is offset against her other income and she saves tax.

The next few years are no better. In fact, she does not sell anything at all. Consequently, she has more losses to claim for. The question is, how long can this go on before it ceases being a proper business and becomes simply an expensive hobby?

The answer depends on how realistic it is for her to make a profit. After all, plenty of businesses are loss-making to start with. Whilst she is still displaying her work and offering it for sale, she will remain in business and can continue claiming losses.

As long as the sales are not contrived in some way (such as orders from relatives) or isolated "flash in the pan" events, the taxman will normally accept that the business is simply being run on an uncommercial basis, rather than being an artificial trade.

The next example is a retired gentleman called Peter who decides to develop his interest in restoring antique clocks into a business. He thinks up a fancy name for the business, buys a domain name, produces an online brochure and registers as self-employed.

Peter spends the first few months travelling to auctions, buying some clocks and studying how the trade works. He does not actually sell anything. His main expenses are the use of his car and the use of his home. Can he claim these as a loss against tax?

Yes he can. Provided he has a real *intention* to sell at a profit he is deemed to be trading and he can claim a loss. However, he would need to be much more active on the selling front if this is to continue. For example, he would need to auction a few items.

Hopefully, the above examples will give you some inspiration on how to turn your hobby into a business. If you are going to end up paying tax on income received from your hobby, then you might as well get tax relief on the costs of that hobby as soon as possible.

Chapter 51

Part-time Businesses: Expenses You Can Claim

In addition to the direct costs of the business, there are various other expenses you might consider claiming against tax.

Spouse/Child Wages

If you have a part-time business, it is fairly common for your partner or children to get involved too, if only on the admin side. A lot of people overlook the fact that you can pay wages to family members and claim them against tax.

Of course, there are some provisos. Firstly, you must actually pay them the wages and be able to prove it. Claiming that they were paid in cash will not cut the mustard. The taxman will want to see cheques or bank transfers to an account in their name.

He will also want to see evidence that the payments were actually wages, such as time-sheets or payslips, so keep a paper trail.

What they actually do with those wages is up to them. As long as there is no express arrangement for the money to be spent in a particular way, they will qualify as genuine payments.

Secondly, they must actually do something *useful* for the business. Best here to keep a log of what they do and why they do it. Try to avoid generic descriptions like research or administration. It must be work that you would have gladly paid someone else to do.

Thirdly, you must not pay them too much. They must be paid no more than the going rate for that type of work or else you will not get a full tax deduction for the payments.

Remember that children under the age of 13 are not usually allowed to work without a council permit. Also, it is even more important to keep proper records of the work young children do, as the taxman would look askance at these payments otherwise.

No need to pay the minimum wage by the way. That does not apply to family members or workers under the age of 16. You can pay your wife or kids 50p an hour if you like. Just don't expect a big present on Father's Day!

Spouse wages are best suited to families where one partner does not have any other earnings or taxable income and consequently does not use up their annual income tax personal allowance. That way, you save tax but they do not have to pay any tax.

If the wages are below the Lower Earnings Limit (£109 per week for 2013/14) **and** your partner has no other jobs or a pension, you do not need to set up a PAYE scheme. Your partner should not need to file a tax return either as no tax will be payable.

Travel Expenses

If you use your own car for business travel, you have a choice of two methods for claiming expenses against tax. You can claim either a fair share of the actual running costs or the approved mileage rates (currently 45p per mile for the first 10,000 miles – 25p above that).

You can also claim additional costs such as parking, road tolls and congestion zone charges, plus a proportion of any loan interest. The loan must have been used specifically to buy the car though.

Usually it will be better to claim a fair share of running costs rather than mileage, mainly because the mileage rates were frozen for so long and did not keep pace with inflation. However, it does mean keeping good records, including all your fuel receipts.

You will need to keep a mileage log, whichever method you use, to keep track of your business travel. Bear in mind here that only journeys that were specifically for business reasons will count, not private journeys where you stopped off to do some errands.

If you claim a proportion of your running costs, you need to work out what that proportion should be. Usually it will be based on your total mileage during the tax year, so if you drive 10,000 miles and 500 were for business, you can claim 5% of your total costs.

You can include all running costs such as fuel, insurance, road tax, maintenance, repairs and breakdown cover. You can even claim an annual capital allowance based on the original cost, although this will depend on the car's CO_2 emissions.

Parking and speeding fines are off-limits by the way. These are not tax deductible even if they were incurred in the course of business.

You can also claim other travel expenses such as train or taxi fares, but you should keep receipts and full details of exactly why you are claiming them. Subsistence is not normally allowed unless you are necessarily absent from home for at least five hours.

Home Expenses

Many people with part-time businesses use their home as an office or a workshop. Sometimes it may be a dedicated room or the garage but often it's just a laptop on the kitchen table. Either way you can claim a reasonable share of your household expenses.

Your claim may not work out at very much, however, as you have to base it not just on the area used but on time spent. Say you work at home on your business for 10 hours a week. Out of 168 hours a week (24 x 7) that is just under 6% of the time.

The area calculation is a bit more generous as you can base it on the number of rooms in your house, even if you only use a small part of that room. Suppose your house has six main rooms and you use one for business. You can claim one-sixth.

Multiply that by the time spent of 6% and you can claim 1% of your relevant household bills. It's not a fortune, as even total bills of £20,000 a year would only yield a £200 expense claim.

If you are a higher-rate taxpayer, that would save you the princely sum of £84 a year in income tax and national insurance. A basic-rate taxpayer would only save £58.

What kind of bills can you claim? Anything to do with the house itself. Mortgage interest, council tax, water rates, insurance, gas, electricity, telephone, internet, cleaning. You can also claim a share of maintenance bills for the house as a whole, or for that room in particular.

You could claim a higher percentage for gas and electricity if you use more power due to working at home. Same goes for telephone or internet, including your mobile or tablet. This can include a share of the line rental or monthly tariff too.

Do not claim anything for the house if you work through your own company though, otherwise it will create a taxable benefit. If the taxman finds out, you will have to pay tax and national insurance on it, and probably penalties too for not declaring it.

Sole traders have an advantage over employees here. If you work through your own company, you will be an employee, subject to strict rules on expenses, but sole traders are self-employed and can claim a fair share of household and motoring costs.

Given the low figures involved, it may be a lot easier just to claim the £4 per week granted by HMRC as a tax-free allowance for working at home. It only comes to £208 per year, but you will not need to keep receipts or do complex calculations.

Employees can claim the £4 per week too (from their employer that is, not the taxman), so it does not matter if you work through your own company.

Financial Costs

If you borrowed money to invest in your business, you cannot claim the loan repayments against tax, but you can claim the interest. Your bank should be able to provide you with a statement showing the split between capital and interest.

It does not matter if the loan was originally for something else. It is the purpose the money is being put to *now* that counts. Like any other expense, the golden rule is that the interest must be *wholly and exclusively for the purposes of the trade.*

The same goes for overdraft interest, bank charges and credit card fees. If these relate solely to an account used for business, they are tax deductible even if the account is not actually in the name of the business.

Chapter 52

Part-time Businesses: Dealing with the Taxman

Registering as Self-Employed

You should tell the taxman as soon as possible when you set up a part-time business, or start treating your hobby as a business. The best way to do that is to register for taxes on the HMRC website:

https://online.hmrc.gov.uk/registration/newbusiness/introduction

Most people should only need to register for self-assessment, not VAT, PAYE or corporation tax.

You will first need to set up a Government Gateway account. This will enable you to file your tax return online. You will be allocated a User ID, asked to give a password and sent a PIN by post.

Once your application goes through, you will be issued with a UTR number (Unique Taxpayer Reference). This is a 10-digit number that will be your main tax identifier from now on.

If you prefer filling out forms and posting them instead, you can use Form CWF1 to register as self-employed. The Post Office should have this form, but you can also download it from here:

www.hmrc.gov.uk/forms/cwf1.pdf

When you register as self-employed you normally have to pay class 2 national insurance contributions too. These are £2.70 per week for 2013/14 but most people pay quarterly by direct debit.

However, if you do not expect the annual income from your business to exceed the class 2 small earnings limit (£5,725 in 2013/14) you can apply for exemption by filling in Form CF10, which you can download from the website address below:

www.hmrc.gov.uk/forms/cf10.pdf

Tax Returns

You will need to complete a tax return every year once you are in the self-assessment system. For online tax returns the deadline is 31 January after the end of the tax year. For paper tax returns you only get until 31 October following the end of the tax year.

If the tax you owe is less than £3,000 HMRC will normally collect it by adjusting your tax code for the following year. They should do this automatically as long as you file your online tax return by 30 December. Otherwise you will have to pay by 31 January.

For paper tax returns the deadline for them to adjust your tax code is 31 October following the end of the tax year. You can download paper tax returns from the HMRC website – no need to ask for one.

Although paper tax returns are still allowed, it really is quicker and easier to file them online. The tax is calculated immediately, so no need to work it out yourself, and the system will prompt you to complete the correct boxes. You can print hard copies too.

The self-employment pages are simplicity itself. No need to attach accounts or analyse expenditure. If your turnover is below £79,000 you only need to enter one figure for your total expenses. No need for a balance sheet either, even though it gives you the option.

You should still keep accounts though to back up the figures. You are required to keep proper accounting records for up to six years, even though you do not need to submit them.

Don't forget to make private use adjustments for things like cars, computer equipment, motor expenses and mobile phones. For a part-time business, these will be quite high as you would expect them to be mainly for your own private use, not the business.

Capital Allowances

If you buy assets such as motor vehicles, computers, printers or smartphones for use in your business, you need to claim them as capital allowances rather than expenses. There is a separate line on the tax return for these.

Every business is entitled to an Annual Investment Allowance. For two years from 1 January 2013 you can claim up to £250,000 per annum for this. After that it goes down to £25,000 per annum, which should still be enough for the average part-time business.

You can use the Annual Investment Allowance for vans and motorcycles but not cars, which are restricted to either 18% of cost for CO_2 emissions up to 130 g/km or 8% above that. This is on a reducing balance basis so it goes down every year.

If you lease a car instead of buying it, you can only claim 85% of the lease rentals against tax if its CO_2 emissions are higher than 130 g/km. This does not apply if you hire a car for 45 days or less.

Until 31 March 2015 you can actually claim 100% of the original cost if CO_2 emissions are 95 g/km or less. However, if you sell the car you will have to pay some of this back as a balancing charge.

Remember that all these capital allowances are subject to the private use restriction, so if business mileage is only 10% of total mileage, you can only claim 10% of the capital allowances.

Class 4 National Insurance

In addition to tax, you may have to pay class 4 national insurance on self-employment profits. This is levied at 9% on profits between £7,755 and £41,450 (2013/14 thresholds) and 2% above that. It is added to your tax bill so a lot of people don't even notice it.

Penalties

If you register for self-assessment and fail to submit a tax return by the required deadline, there is an automatic £100 fine, even if you do not owe any tax. However, if you register late, you always get at least three months to file a tax return, either online or on paper.

After three months they can start charging £10 per day for each day you are late (up to 90 days) with another £300 penalty kicking in after six months (or 5% of the tax owed if this is greater). You can see how important it is not to be late with your tax return!

If tax is paid late there will also be automatic surcharges. These kick in at 5% if the tax is more than 28 days late, followed by another 5% if it is six months late. After 12 months there is another 5% so the total surcharges could be 15% of the tax owed.

Combined with the late filing penalty, you could be fined at least 20% of the tax owed if you are more than a year late. It could even exceed 100% of tax owed in the more extreme cases.

On top of this, there are also penalties for failing to notify HMRC that you are self-employed. You must do this by 5th October following the end of the tax year or there will be penalties for each year of assessment in which the failure to notify continues.

Penalties are based on a percentage of "potential lost revenue". In effect, this means the tax and class 4 national insurance payable. The penalties vary according to the seriousness of the failure, whether or not your disclosure was "prompted" by HMRC and when you finally got round to telling them.

For example, a penalty for deliberate concealment would start at 100% of potential lost revenue whereas a so-called non-deliberate failure would start at 30% of potential lost revenue. However, penalties can be reduced, suspended or even cancelled according to the degree of co-operation given.

You can also avoid a penalty if you have a "reasonable excuse". The law does not define the word "reasonable" so it takes its ordinary dictionary meaning. HMRC think that it means exceptional circumstances but the tax tribunals say otherwise!

It is always worth appealing if you think you have a reasonable excuse, firstly to HMRC and if necessary to the Tribunal.

Choosing a Year End

You can choose any date you like for your year end. It does not have to be 5 April or 31 December. You normally specify the year end when you complete your first tax return for the business. Your year end can make a big difference to your tax bill. Speak to an accountant about this so you can make an informed decision. It will determine the basis period on which your tax is assessed.

Part 9

Domestic Tax Matters

Chapter 53

Hiring a Nanny

Many parents work full-time and hire a nanny to look after their children until they get home. She is usually paid a fixed weekly sum, often in cash. For some odd historical reason, nanny pay is often agreed on a **net** basis, not gross like the rest of us.

Many people don't realise that they are employers in this situation and are responsible for deducting PAYE from the nanny's wages. Even worse, they fail to appreciate that tax and national insurance contributions are based on their deemed gross pay, not net pay.

If you employ a nanny, you must abide by the rules and take your responsibilities as an employer seriously. Otherwise, it is best to use a nursery, a nanny agency or a registered childminder.

Calculating Your Nanny's Tax

You will need to gross up your nanny's pay to work out tax and national insurance. Here are the tax and national insurance figures (2013/14 rates) at various levels of pay:

	£	£	£	£	£	£	£	£
Weekly wages	**150**	**200**	**250**	**300**	**350**	**400**	**450**	**500**
Gross equivalent	150	215	288	361	435	508	582	656
Income tax	0	7	21	36	51	65	80	95
Employee NI	0	8	17	25	34	43	52	61
Employer NI	0	9	19	30	40	50	60	70
Weekly PAYE	0	24	57	91	125	158	192	226
Quarterly PAYE	0	312	741	1183	1625	2054	2496	2938
Quarterly wages	1950	2600	3250	3900	4550	5200	5850	6500
Total cost	**1950**	**2912**	**3991**	**5083**	**6175**	**7254**	**8346**	**9438**

You only have to pay HMRC quarterly in arrears, but you must pay them by the 22nd of the month following the calendar quarter. If paying by cheque, it must actually clear by the 22nd. Note that a PAYE month always starts on the 6th and ends on the 5th.

What if My Nanny Has Another Job?

If your nanny works for other parents or has a job in the evening, it is possible you could pay even more tax and national insurance. It depends on which employer has her tax code.

Only one employer at a time can use her tax code. The other employers must deduct tax at 20% from her gross pay. As the table below shows (2013/14 rates), the PAYE bill increases substantially.

	£	£	£	£	£	£	£	£
Weekly wages	**150**	**200**	**250**	**300**	**350**	**400**	**450**	**500**
Gross equivalent	194	268	341	415	489	562	635	709
Income tax	39	54	68	83	98	112	127	142
Employee NI	5	14	23	32	41	50	58	67
Employer NI	6	17	27	37	47	57	67	77
Weekly PAYE	50	85	118	152	186	219	252	286
Quarterly PAYE	650	1105	1534	1976	2418	2847	3276	3718
Quarterly wages	1950	2600	3250	3900	4550	5200	5850	6500
Total cost	**2600**	**3705**	**4784**	**5876**	**6968**	**8047**	**9126**	**10218**

So which employer gets to use her tax code? Whichever one employs her first. If your nanny gives you a P45 from her previous employer or ticks the box on a P46 stating that she has no other jobs, that allows you to use her tax code.

If she does not give you a P45 or a P46, or she ticks the box on a P46 stating that she has another job (or a pension if you hire an old lady) then you must operate a 'BR' code and deduct 20% tax on the **whole** of her equivalent gross pay.

This obviously isn't fair on you, so if you are in this situation the nanny should accept a lower wage. After all, if she had a second job anywhere else, she would take home less money after tax than if it was her only job.

Either that or she should ask HMRC to switch her tax code to you, but this may take time and her pay will have to be adjusted later.

Speaking of old ladies, people over state pension age do not have to pay national insurance contributions (although their employers do) so this might reduce your PAYE bill a bit, although the saving should be passed on to the nanny in all fairness.

What about Student Loans?

If your nanny went to university it is highly likely she will have a student loan. In that case, if she earns more than a certain amount, you will have to deduct student loan repayments.

The rate is 9% on all **gross** pay over and above £314 per week (2013/14 limit). This must be paid to HMRC quarterly along with her tax and national insurance.

HMRC will send you Form SL1 if you need to deduct student loan. You also need to do so if there is a Y in Box 5 on her P45.

Can My Nanny be Self-Employed?

Almost certainly not. Usually, only registered childminders are allowed to be self-employed. They work from their own homes, not yours, and must be registered with Ofsted in England or the Care Inspectorate in Scotland.

In rare cases, HMRC do allow some nannies to be self-employed, but it is not automatic that this status passes from job to job, and you would need to ask HMRC for a ruling (in writing).

If a nanny tells you that she is self-employed and gives you a UTR number, take it with a pinch of salt. A UTR is not conclusive evidence that she is self-employed. Unless she runs a business and has lots of other clients, you will be deemed her employer.

The only other option is to use a nanny agency and let them pay her. They will then be her employer, not you, and will be responsible for operating PAYE on her earnings. Obviously this will cost more though and is best suited to temporary nannies.

If you want to pay the nanny yourself, you have no choice but to set up a PAYE scheme and operate a payroll for her. This means paying tax and national insurance, giving her payslips and reporting her wages to HMRC every time you pay her.

The only time you do not have to do this is if you pay her less than £109 per week (2013/14 rate) **and** she has no other work. This is unlikely unless you employ your nanny for 17 hours a week or less and only pay her the minimum wage (£6.31 per hour).

How Do I Set Up a PAYE Scheme?

This is really easy. There are two ways you can do it. You can either phone the New Employer Helpline on 0300 200 3211 or you can visit the HMRC website page below and register for taxes:

https://online.hmrc.gov.uk/registration/newbusiness/introduction

Of course, you are not really a new business, but it is the same process for people employing domestic staff as it is for businesses.

The trouble with the online method is that you need a UTR number. Most people who are themselves employees will not have one, so you either need to register for self-assessment, which may well be totally unnecessary, or phone the above helpline.

Either way, you will need to open a Government Gateway account so you can file online. This will give you a user ID and password (of your choice). Then you have to wait for an activation PIN to turn up in the post.

Once your PAYE scheme has been set up (you will get a letter with two reference numbers) you can register it as an online service. To do this, log on to your Government Gateway account, click on "Services You Can Add" and select "PAYE for Employers".

Enter the two reference numbers for your PAYE scheme and your post code, wait for yet another activation PIN to turn up in the post, and away you go. You are ready to start filing online.

If all that sounds very long-winded, you could always go to a payroll agency and they will set up a PAYE scheme for you as part of their service, but obviously it will cost more to use an agency.

How Do I Run a Payroll for My Nanny?

You've got two choices here – either do it yourself or use a payroll agency. There are plenty of payroll agencies specialising in nannies (and other domestic staff) and their fees are fairly low – about £250 a year on average.

This includes not just the payroll service but setting up a PAYE scheme and providing a template employment contract. You could also go to an accountant but they will probably charge more and not provide such a comprehensive service.

If you decide to do it yourself, your best bet is to download the free HMRC Basic PAYE Tools as your payroll software and use this to calculate your PAYE liabilities. It can also make the new Real Time Information (RTI) submissions to HMRC each time you pay your nanny.

What it won't do is work out the gross wage if you pay your nanny net. You will have to work this out yourself and enter the gross figure in PAYE Tools. You could ask an accountant to work this out for you. It's only a few minutes' work so shouldn't cost much.

It is very important to comply with the new RTI rules on paying employees, because there will be penalties for late reporting of employee wages from 6 April 2014. You must make a Full Payment Submission on or before the date you pay your nanny.

There will also be penalties if you are late paying your quarterly PAYE bills. You are allowed one late payment but repeated failures will incur higher and higher penalties. These will not be imposed until after the end of the tax year, so they could come as a shock.

Is My Nanny Entitled to Statutory Holiday?

Yes, they are employees and entitled to the same employment rights as everyone else. Statutory holiday is 28 days a year (including the eight bank holidays). If we have an extra bank holiday (to celebrate a Royal Wedding for example) it remains 28 days.

If the nanny does not work full-time, she is only allowed a pro-rata number of days or hours. You always multiply by 5.6 to calculate holiday entitlement. For example, 15 hours a week would allow her 84 hours statutory holiday per annum.

Hours are translated into days according to how many hours she works in a day. For example, if she works 60 hours a week over five days she gets either 28 days or 336 hours, but the hours would be based on a 12-hour day, so she would still only get 28 days.

However, she can never get more than 28 days even if she works more than five days a week. Say she works 60 hours a week over six days. She would still get 336 hours but spread over 28 days.

If statutory holiday works out at a fraction of a day you can either round it up to the nearest whole day or work out the exact number of hours for the odd day. You can never round down.

You are allowed to specify when your nanny takes her statutory leave. For example, you could insist that it includes the week between Christmas and New Year, or when you yourself go on holiday. However, this needs to be in her employment contract.

You also do not have to let her take bank holidays off or pay her for bank holidays, although most parents would insist that she does as they would be at home themselves on those days. Again, it needs to be in her employment contract.

If your nanny does not take her full statutory holiday, you must pay her in lieu or allow her to carry it forward to the next holiday year. You can decide when a holiday year starts and finishes. If she leaves, any unused holiday must be added to her final pay.

Equally, if she has taken too much holiday when she leaves, you are entitled to deduct it from her final pay. Either way, it is good practice to show holiday adjustments separately on her payslip. It must also be paid at her usual rate of pay.

Is My Nanny Entitled to Statutory Maternity Pay?

Yes, although she must qualify for it as prescribed by law. That means she must have worked for you continuously for at least 26 weeks going into the Qualifying Week (QW). She must normally give you at least 28 days notice of her maternity leave too.

The QW is the 15th week before the baby is due, as shown on Form MAT1B or some other form of medical evidence signed by her doctor or midwife. You must see this before you can pay her SMP and it must be dated no earlier than 20 weeks before the baby is due.

Your nanny is entitled to commence her maternity leave from the 11th week before the baby is due (unless he/she is born earlier).

She can take up to 52 weeks off in total, and you have to keep her job open all that time unless she officially resigns.

She can have up to 10 "Keeping in Touch" days which you must pay her for. In fact, you have to give her a whole day's pay even if she only works for an hour or less on these days. If she works more than 10 days, her SMP will not be paid for that week.

SMP will stop when your nanny officially returns to work or if she is employed by someone else after the baby is born. She must give you eight weeks' notice if her return to work date changes.

SMP is payable for up to 39 weeks. For the first six weeks it is paid at 90% of her average weekly earnings for the eight-week period leading up to her Qualifying Week. After six weeks it goes down to £136.78 per week (2013/14 rate) or stays at 90% of her average weekly earnings if that is lower.

SMP is taxable and must go through the payroll. You must only pay your nanny the net amount after deducting tax and national insurance. However, you do not have to pay her weekly. You could pay it monthly if you wish.

As a small employer, you are entitled to recover all her SMP from HMRC. In fact, you get an extra 3% on top of this to cover you for employer's national insurance, even if you don't actually pay any. Therefore, you could even make a small profit out of it.

You can apply for advance funding from HMRC for your nanny's maternity pay. You can do this online if it is in the same tax year. Otherwise you will have to write to them. As SMP for 39 weeks is likely to cost around £7,000 it is highly advisable to do this.

To obtain a refund for SMP already paid in a previous tax year, you need to complete Form SP32 and send it to HMRC in Newcastle.

Once your nanny has told you she is pregnant, shown you Form MAT1B and given you 28 days' notice, you must confirm in writing the date her maternity leave will start and when it will finish. You must also confirm how much SMP she will be paid for that period.

If your nanny is not eligible for SMP for some reason, you must give her Form SMP1 instead. She can then apply to Jobcentre Plus for Maternity Allowance, although to qualify for this she must have worked at least 26 weeks during a 66-week test period.

Incidentally, a nanny could also get Statutory Adoption Pay or even, believe it or not, Statutory Paternity Pay. The latter could apply if she is a lesbian and her partner already claims SMP.

If your nanny resigns during her maternity leave or states that she will not be returning to work, you still have to pay her SMP for the maximum 39 weeks but no longer need to keep her job open.

Whatever you do, you must not dismiss your nanny for being pregnant or taking maternity leave or she will have a cast-iron case against you at an Employment Tribunal.

Pregnant women are also entitled to paid time off for antenatal care and special health and safety protection in the workplace. If you don't know what this might entail, it is best to consult the health and safety officers at your local council.

These are just the bare bones of the subject. If you want to know more about SMP or maternity leave, consult HMRC Helpbook E15. You can download a free copy from the webpage below:

www.hmrc.gov.uk/helpsheets/e15.pdf

After reading all this, you might be tempted to employ an older woman who is not likely to fall pregnant (or a male nanny if you can find one) but beware of breaching the age discrimination laws.

Is My Nanny Entitled to Statutory Sick Pay?

Yes, they are entitled to the same SSP as other employees. The good news here is that you can recover it from the Government by deducting it from your quarterly PAYE bills.

You do not have to pay your nanny any wages for sick leave (unless you agreed to do so in her employment contract or statement of particulars) but you must pay her SSP if she qualifies.

SPP kicks in after a period of sickness lasting four days or more. This includes weekends, bank holidays and non-working days.

Once she has been ill for four days, then you have to pay SSP for all Qualifying Days except the first three of them.

Qualifying Days are days your nanny would have worked had she not been ill, including those within the first four days of absence. The first three are known as Waiting Days. You do not have to pay her SSP for those. If you do, it will not be recoverable.

For example, if your nanny normally works Mondays to Fridays except Wednesdays and is ill from Friday to Thursday, you only have to pay SSP for one day (Thursday) as Friday, Monday and Tuesday are Waiting Days and Wednesday is not a Qualifying Day.

However, periods of sickness are linked if the gap between them is eight weeks or less. In that case, there only need to be three Waiting Days for the whole period of sickness. They may well have been served during the first period of sickness, so SSP may kick in straight away.

This remains the case even if the nanny was absent for unrelated conditions. For example, she could be off sick one week with a broken ankle and off again six weeks later with the flu. However, each sickness period must last at least four days to qualify.

The weekly rate of SSP (2013/14) is **£86.70**. Divide by the number of Qualifying Days in that week for single days. It should be paid on the normal pay dates and go though the payroll on top of wages, deducting tax and national insurance.

Your nanny must notify you of her sickness within seven days of the first Qualifying Day. You can require medical evidence like a doctor's note but this is not obligatory. You can let her self-certify sickness periods of up to seven days if you wish using Form SC2.

If your nanny produces a "fit note" from her doctor stating that she is able to undertake lighter duties or work fewer hours than normal, you do not have to accept this if it does not suit you. In that case, it would count as a period of sickness for SSP.

SSP is payable for a maximum of 28 weeks, either in a single period of sickness or linked periods of sickness. When SSP comes to an end you must give your nanny Form SSP1 within seven days.

You must keep records of all dates of sickness lasting four consecutive days or more, all payments of SSP and any unpaid SSP (with reasons) for at least three years from the end of the tax year.

No SSP can be paid if the nanny's average earnings in the eight weeks leading up to the first Qualifying Day are less than £109 per week. That is not likely to be the case unless she works two days a week or less.

These are the bare bones of the SSP rules. For full details, you need to consult HMRC Helpbook E14. You can download a free copy of this from the webpage below:

www.hmrc.gov.uk/helpsheets/e14.pdf

Lastly, it is worth bearing in mind that an employee who falls sick whilst he/she is on holiday can insist that it is treated as sick leave instead and take the holiday again later.

Do I Have to Pay My Nanny a Pension?

Not yet. You may have heard about workplace pensions and the fact that employers are now obliged to contribute towards them. The bad news is that this also applies to employers of nannies and other domestic staff.

However, the good news is that this will not come in until November 2015 at the earliest. The exact date depends on your PAYE reference but it may be as late as April 2017.

You can look up your staging date on the table published by the Pensions Regulator, which you can look up on the webpage below:

www.thepensionsregulator.gov.uk/employers/staging-date-timeline.aspx

However, all employers will receive at least 12 months' notice, and they will get a further letter three months before they are due to enrol their workers into a pension scheme, so plenty of warning.

How much will you have to pay? Well that depends on both their earnings and the percentage applicable at the time. At the moment employers are only required to contribute 1% of gross earnings. This goes up to 2% in October 2017 and 3% in October 2018.

You do not have to pay this on all their earnings, however. At present, it is only wages between the upper and lower earnings limits for national insurance that qualify for contributions. For 2013/14, this band is £5,668 to £41,450.

The pension obligation will only be triggered if your nanny earns at least £9,440 (2013/14). We can assume that most nannies will earn at least that much. The more relevant figure is her age, as it is only workers aged 22 or over that have to be enrolled.

The nanny herself will have to contribute too. Until October 2018 her contribution will be the same as the employer. After that it will be 4%. The nanny's contribution will attract a 25% Government top-up, so total contributions will be 8% by October 2018.

You can choose which pension scheme the contributions are paid into. The Government has set up a new pension scheme for auto-enrolment called NEST (National Employment Savings Trust).

Tax relief on an employer's pension contribution is normally given by a reduction in the corporation tax they pay on their profits, but of course, parents don't make profits on their kids, so no tax relief will be given on their contributions to the nanny's pension.

The best solution for this would be for the government to allow a top-up on the parent's contributions too. We wait with interest to see if the Government allows this. It would be unfair if they didn't.

Auto-enrolment is not entirely mandatory as the employee has a month to opt out. If your nanny opts out, then neither of you will need to make any contributions.

However, you are not allowed to put any pressure on your nanny to opt out, nor must you offer her any inducements to do so. It will be interesting to see how they are going to police that one!

Can I Give My Nanny Benefits-in-Kind?

Yes, you can give her tax-free benefits such as a mobile phone or pension contributions, or taxable ones such as a car, gym membership, health insurance or shopping vouchers. The latter must be reported to HMRC on an annual P11D.

That does not mean she will pay more tax just because you let her drive the family car though. It's only if it is made available to her for private use too, such as driving to work in the morning.

Bear in mind that HMRC may deal with benefits-in-kind by adjusting her tax code for next year rather than asking her to pay the tax. You know what that means – a higher PAYE bill – and guess who's going to pay that!

All things considered, benefits-in-kind for nannies are more trouble than they are worth, unless you're sure they are tax-free.

Can I Pay My Nanny Expenses?

Yes, but you have to be careful. It is OK to give her some money to spend on the kids, as long as she gives you the change. Otherwise, you would have to put it through the payroll. It may seem very pedantic, but otherwise it is tantamount to cash-in-hand wages.

The same goes for petrol money if she uses her own car. You can only pay her mileage for the actual distance travelled in the course of her duties. The maximum rate is 45p per mile. Any more than this and it has to go through the payroll.

Also, do not pay her mileage expenses for travelling between home and work, as this is "ordinary commuting" and is not tax free. It will be taxable as cash wages if you do, and you will have to gross it up for the payroll too as you'll be deemed to have paid her net.

What about Au Pairs?

If you hire an au pair rather than a nanny, there are two important differences for tax purposes. Firstly, you do not have to pay them the minimum wage. However, this is only true if they live in your home as a member of the family.

In that case, you will be providing them with accommodation and paying for their board, so a lower wage would be fair anyway. Plus you will be expected to give them a couple of days a week off and help them learn English.

Secondly, if you don't pay them more than the lower earnings limit (£109 per week for 2013/14) **and** they do not work for anyone else, then you don't have to set up a PAYE scheme or deduct tax and national insurance.

What about Other Domestic Staff?

It is not just nannies you might find yourself employing. You may also employ a cleaner, gardener, care worker or someone else who tends to work only for you and is not self-employed. In that case, exactly the same rules will apply to them.

Of course, these people are more likely to be self-employed due to the nature of their work. Houses and gardens don't tend to require as much time to look after as kids, so cleaners and gardeners have more scope to work for others as well as you.

Even so, it is in your own interests to make sure they really are self-employed and that you cannot be seen as their employer. This becomes more likely the more often they work for you.

How Does this Help Me Save Tax?

Well it doesn't really! The only reason this subject is covered in a book about tax saving is because it may help you decide whether it is worth having both parents go out to work or if one of you might as well stay at home and look after the kids.

Therefore, you should work out how much extra income you will have after paying the nanny **and** her tax and decide if it is worth it or not, given all the other factors you need to consider.

The new Government childcare vouchers scheme (which will be introduced in autumn 2015) may be highly relevant to this decision as, to qualify, both parents must be working.

Chapter 54

Taking on a Lodger

It often makes good financial sense to take on a lodger. You might need a bit of extra cash to help make ends meet, or to save up for a dream holiday or a new car, and if you have a spare room that isn't used for anything else, why not put it to good use?

In legal terms, a lodger has very few rights compared to a tenant as they are living in your home under a licence agreement, not an assured short-hold tenancy. To discover more, check out relevant websites such as www.landlordzone.co.uk

There are several issues to consider when taking on a lodger, but this book is about tax-saving tactics, so we will focus solely on the tax implications. The main thing to remember is that rent from a lodger is taxable, unless you make use of the Rent-a-Room scheme.

Tax relief under Rent-a-Room is given automatically, so you do not need to apply for it or tick a box on your tax return. In fact, you do not need to fill in a tax return at all unless HMRC ask you to. However, you do need to keep proper records of rent received.

Under Rent-a-Room, the first £4,250 of rent you get from lodgers is tax free. That equates to just over £350 per calendar month, which is not a huge sum for furnished accommodation these days. It also includes any extra payments you get for cooking, laundry, etc.

That £4,250 limit has been frozen now since 1997, so it has lost a lot of value since the scheme was first introduced back in 1992. Also, if the property is in joint names, you only get £2,125 each, although in that case the rent would be split between you.

Bear in mind that the £4,250 limit is based on rent **due** for the period of occupation, not on rent paid. You can't get round it by manipulating the payments, e.g. by advancing or delaying them.

When you assess rent receivable against the £4,250 limit, you must base it on the amount that was actually due for the tax year, regardless of whether it was all paid or not. Rent arrears can be deducted but only if they are written off once and for all.

In that case, you should keep a record of any bad debts on the rent as you must be able to prove that it was no longer recoverable.

Of course, you can still charge your lodger a deposit to be held against any damages or missed rent payments (in fact you would be very unwise not to). This will not count as rental income unless you end up keeping it once the lodger has gone.

If total payments from your lodgers exceed £4,250 in the tax year, you are only taxed on the excess under Rent-a-Room. For example, if the rent comes to £5,000 you will pay tax on £750. A basic-rate taxpayer would pay £150 and a higher-rate taxpayer £300.

However, there is a *quid pro quo* with the Rent-a-Room scheme in that you are not allowed to claim any expenses against tax. Normally you can deduct certain expenses against rent from a lodger such as a share of household bills or 10% wear and tear, but not if you use this scheme.

That means you may not actually be better off claiming tax relief under the Rent-a-Room scheme at all. For example, suppose rent is £5,000 but you incur expenses of £4,500. You should be taxed on £500, but under Rent-a-Room you would pay tax on £750.

In that instance, you would be better off opting out of the scheme for that year, or not claiming tax relief under it in the first place. This often happens in the first year of letting when a householder may incur one-off costs such as legal fees for rent agreements.

Therefore, it may benefit you to be outside the scheme to start with but then opt in later. Alternatively, you could claim tax relief under the scheme to start with but then opt out if expenses start going up and you would be better off outside.

However, if you do this you must tell the taxman by 31 January of the year after next following the end of the tax year. That gives you 22 months (minus five days). The only exception is if rents are less than £4,250 in which case the scheme applies automatically.

Incidentally, if you often have more than one lodger at a time, you may lose part of your CGT exemption when you sell the house. To avoid this, let the lodgers have the run of the house and make them do household chores too. Then it will clearly be a house-share, not a letting business.

You would not normally expect to make a loss by having a lodger (unless they were very dirty and you spent a fortune on cleaning), but if you do you can carry forward the loss and claim it against future rents, even if you subsequently claim the exemption.

Extra payments by the lodger only count as rent if they are for services provided. If a lodger merely shares the household bills (on a fair and equitable basis) then it does not count towards rent.

There are a few qualifying conditions for the Rent-a-Room scheme:

- Your property must be your only or main residence,
- The lodgings must be let for residential purposes only,
- The lodgings must be properly furnished,
- The lodgings must not be self-contained accommodation,
- The lodger must not run a business from the property,
- The scheme does not apply to companies or partnerships

These conditions are worth looking at in a bit more detail.

Only or Main Residence

The interesting point to note here is that this is not exactly the same test that applies for capital gains tax purposes should you have more than one property. In fact, it may not even be the same property as the one you nominate as your main residence.

The rule for Rent-a-Room is a bit stricter. You don't have to live under the same roof as your lodger all the time, but HMRC would expect you to live there **most** of the time. It should be the place where people would normally expect to find you.

However, it only needs to be your main residence at some time during the tax year. How long you have to live there will depend on the facts in each case, but for it to be a residence at all there must be some degree of permanence to the arrangement.

A weekend home would probably qualify if you live there on a regular basis. So would a home you live in during the week (to be close to your job for instance) or homes you occupy for more or less equal lengths of time as part of your general lifestyle.

However, a holiday home would not qualify as it is not occupied on a regular basis. Likewise, if you only live in the property for a brief period, it is unlikely to qualify for Rent-a-Room as it was clearly never intended to be your permanent home.

Your occupation of the property must be simultaneous at some point with the letting itself for Rent-a-Room to apply. For instance, it would not qualify if it ceased before the letting began or only started after the letting ceased. The bottom line is that you need to be careful with long absences.

Residential Lodgings

This speaks for itself really. Rent-a-Room relief is not allowed if the letting is for a store room, an office or some other non-residential purpose. The lodgings must be primarily for residential use.

However, this does not preclude the use of a room for studying or similar activities, so long as it was incidental to living there. Therefore, a student would qualify for Rent-a-Room relief.

Furnished Accommodation

There is no legal definition of furnished property so its ordinary dictionary meaning must apply. For Rent-a-Room, the standard is a bit lower as lettings must not be self-contained. As a bare minimum, it should include carpets, curtains, a bed and storage.

A kitchen, bathroom and toilet should also be available, at least on a shared basis, equipped with facilities for cooking, washing and cleaning. You should also provide hot and cold running water, electricity, lighting, and an adequate heating system.

The type and size of the lettings is not prescribed by the tax rules but of course they must be habitable and large enough to be suitably furnished. That would tend to rule out large cupboards or outhouses unless they had been suitably renovated.

And if the 18th century tradition of keeping a hermit at the bottom of your garden ever came back into fashion, it probably wouldn't qualify for Rent-a-Room relief. Especially if you kept him in a cave!

Self-contained Accommodation

This is another term that is not prescribed by the tax rules, but HMRC has provided some guidance here on page PIM4004 of their Property Income Manual. This deals with whether a property has been split up into more than one residence.

Sometimes this is obvious, as in an external granny flat with its own separate entrance. However, sometimes a separate residence may be part of the same building. For example, a basement flat with its own kitchen and bathroom could well be self-contained.

However, if the building was originally built as a single residence and the division into separate residences is only temporary, you can still claim Rent-a-Room relief. Whether it is temporary or not will depend on a number of factors.

For example, how long has the property been divided and are there any plans to remove the division? Would it be necessary to make structural alterations? Does the flat have its own external entrance or postal address? Does it have its own electricity supply?

Most basements and attics are readily convertible and do not have a separate address or mains services, so you can usually put lodgers in them without falling foul of the Rent-a-Room rules even if they have their own kitchens and en-suite bathrooms.

Business Use

Although the Rent-a-Room rules state that the letting must be for residential use, this does not rule out any business use whatsoever. So long as the residence is not used as a *place* of business, the lodger can still run a business from home.

This is becoming far more common these days and should not interfere with the Rent-a-Room rules. So long as the lodgings are *primarily* for residential purposes, there is nothing to stop the lodger having a desk and computer in there for business use.

However, using the lodgings for storage or for anything other than simple admin tasks is a different matter. For example, the lodger could not use it as a treatment room for his patients or as a warehouse for his stock, even if he still chose to live there.

Recent/Future Tax Changes

Almost every year the Budget brings new developments to the tax landscape and 2013 was no exception. There were quite a few changes that will be of interest to the average salary earner. Many will not come into force until 2014 or even later.

New Childcare Vouchers

This was by far the most important announcement, at least as far as working parents are concerned. From autumn 2015 (the exact date is yet to be announced) working parents will be able to claim vouchers worth up to £1,200 a year for each qualifying child.

How the Vouchers Will Work

The vouchers will only be available where both parents (or a single parent) work at least 16 hours a week. If one parent does not work (and they both have parental responsibility) then they cannot apply for the childcare vouchers.

Parents claiming tax credits or universal credit will not qualify for the scheme either. Instead, they will get a big increase in the level of childcare costs qualifying for support. This is planned to go up to 85% by April 2016.

Both employees and the self-employed will qualify for the new scheme. However, any person whose total income exceeds £150,000 per annum will not qualify (so a couple on £150,000 a year each will be fine!).

It is expected that parents will buy online vouchers from existing providers and, for every 80p they spend, the Government will provide a 20p top-up. The maximum top-up per child will be £1,200 (if the parents spend £4,800) so the vouchers would be worth £6,000.

To start with, only children under five will qualify. However, it is planned that all children under 12 will qualify by about 2020. The vouchers will be available for any form of regulated childcare, not just nurseries, and so extra-curricular activities will qualify.

Regulated childcare means the provider must be approved by OFSTED in England or the equivalent bodies in the rest of the UK. Therefore, unregistered nannies or au pairs will not qualify.

What if I Get Childcare Support from My Employer?

You cannot receive both employer support and the new Government scheme vouchers. You must choose which one you prefer to have.

You can join a childcare scheme run by your employer right up to the date the new Government scheme is rolled out. However, from that date onwards, you no longer have a choice. If you are not in an employer scheme by then, it will be too late to join one. You will have to use the Government scheme instead.

Which Scheme Is Best?

This will depend on the following factors:

- Whether the employer scheme is free or salary sacrifice
- How many children you have
- The age of your children
- How much you earn (or will be earning)
- How much salary you sacrifice for vouchers
- How much you plan to spend on childcare
- Whether you are a higher-rate taxpayer
- Whether or not both of you can get employer childcare

Firstly, if your employer gives you vouchers free on top of your normal salary, without requiring you to sacrifice any salary, normally it would be worth keeping them.

If your employer offers a free workplace crèche without requiring any salary sacrifice, that would be worth using as it saves you the cost and inconvenience of having to use a nursery. Of course, it depends on the quality of the childcare provision too.

The main advantage of the new Government scheme is that you can claim vouchers for *each* qualifying child, whereas the existing employer schemes do not reflect the number of children. On the other hand, employer schemes are open to both parents individually.

The Government scheme is only open to both parents together, not individually, and they must both work at least 16 hours per week, otherwise they will not qualify for the new vouchers. This obviously rules out mothers who stay at home.

Clearly, the Government scheme favours larger families, but only for children aged up to five years (initially), whilst childcare vouchers provided by your employer are valid up to 1 September following your child's 15th birthday (16th if disabled).

The Government scheme only saves you 20% of the total cost (the basic tax rate) whilst higher-rate taxpayers can save tax at 40% or 45% (provided they joined an employer scheme by 6th April 2011). You also save on national insurance contributions.

If you earn more than £150,000 a year you will not qualify for the Government scheme at all, whereas existing employer schemes have no upper limit. In that case, you will not have a choice. You will have to stick with your employer's scheme.

Income is also relevant for child benefit purposes. You can use a salary sacrifice scheme to stay below the £50,000 threshold, whilst the new Government scheme will not enable you to do this. You need to factor the additional tax into the equation.

Childcare vouchers (or direct contracts) are restricted to £243 per month for basic-rate taxpayers (or higher-rate taxpayers who joined by 6th April 2011). Therefore, the maximum you can get is £2,916 per parent, compared to £6,000 per child.

If you work through your own company, you can take vouchers worth up to £243 per month on top of your salary, tax free. These will qualify for relief against corporation tax at 20%, so if both parents get them, this could save you £1,166 each year.

It also depends on how much you expect to spend on childcare. Many people may not be able to afford £6,000 per child, in which case they will forego much of the tax benefits. The other factors may then come into play more.

Lastly, you need to keep one eye on the future, as you will be spending money on your children for a long time after they cease needing nursery care. Teenagers can be expensive, so bear in mind the Government scheme will only be for children aged under 12.

Even then, that age limit may not come in until 2020. No announcements have been made on how it will be phased in yet. Your children may always be just that bit too old for the Government scheme if the new age limit is phased in gradually.

Case Study # 1

Jim and Jane have two children aged four and six. Jane works 16 hours a week and Jim works full-time. They spend £5,000 a year on childcare, of which £4,000 is for the youngest child and £1,000 for the oldest.

Jim earns £40,000 per annum and his employer offers a salary sacrifice scheme for childcare vouchers. Jim has always taken the vouchers but it is now late 2015. Should he continue with the salary sacrifice arrangement or join the Government scheme?

The tax and national insurance figures below are based on 2013/14 rates:

	Employer Scheme	Government Scheme
Annual salary	£37,084	£40,000
Income tax	- £5,527	- £6,110
National Insurance	- £3,520	- £3,870
Net salary	£28,037	£30,020
Childcare vouchers	+£2,916	-
Total net income	£30,953	£30,020
Cost of new vouchers	-	- £4,000
Government top-up	-	+£800
Childcare costs	- £5,000	- £1,000
Disposable income	£25,953	£25,820
Additional income	+£133	

In this example, we can see that Jim and Jane are £133 a year better off sticking with the employer scheme.

This is a very marginal result and is affected mainly by the overall childcare costs and the allocation between the two children. If they spent another £700 on the youngest child, it would swing in favour of the new scheme as they would save an extra £140.

Note that Jane's income is not factored in as this will be the same whichever scheme is chosen. It is not relevant to this decision.

Some employers may also partially subsidise the salary sacrifice arrangement by ploughing their own national insurance savings into the scheme. In that case, the equation could well swing a lot more in favour of the employer's scheme.

Case Study # 2

Janet and John have two children aged three and four. Janet works for 16 hours a week and John works full-time. They spend £8,000 a year on childcare – £4,000 for each child.

John earns £40,000 per annum and his employer offers a salary sacrifice scheme for childcare vouchers. John has always taken the vouchers but it is now late 2015. Should he continue with the salary sacrifice arrangement or join the Government scheme?

The tax and national insurance figures below are based on 2013/14 rates:

	Employer Scheme	Government Scheme
Annual salary	£37,084	£40,000
Income tax	- £5,527	- £6,110
National Insurance	- £3,520	- £3,870
Net salary	£28,037	£30,020
Childcare vouchers	+£2,916	-
Total net income	£30,953	£30,020
Cost of new vouchers	-	- £8,000
Government top-up	-	+£1,600
Childcare costs	- £8,000	-
Disposable income	+£22,953	+£23,620
Additional income		+£667

Now the equation swings in favour of the Government scheme by £667 a year. Childcare costs are higher and both children qualify. The £800 additional tax relief is what makes the difference.

Bear in mind, however, that the children will not qualify for long. Once they are five years old all the tax relief will disappear, and then Janet and John will be £933 a year worse off.

The key here is how much money Janet and John intend to spend on childcare in future years, and how soon the Government puts the age limit up. They risk making a short-term saving on nursery care only to lose much more later when the tax relief runs out.

Case Study # 3

Jack and Jill have four children aged two, four, six and eight. They both work full-time and earn £50,000 per annum each. They spend a total of £15,000 a year on childcare – £5,000 for each of the two youngest children, £3,000 on the six-year-old and £2,000 on the eldest child.

Their employers both offer salary sacrifice schemes for childcare vouchers. They have always taken the vouchers but it is now late 2015. Should they continue with the salary sacrifice arrangements or join the Government scheme?

The tax and national insurance figures below are based on 2013/14 rates:

	Employer Scheme	Government Scheme
Annual salaries	£94,168	£100,000
Income tax	- £21,087	- £23,420
National Insurance	- £8,313	- £8,429
Net salaries	£64,768	£68,151
Childcare vouchers	+£5,832	-
Total net income	£70,600	£68,151
Cost of new vouchers	-	- £10,000
Government top-up	-	+£2,000
Childcare costs	- £15,000	- £5,000
Disposable income	+£55,600	+£55,151
Additional income	+£449	

Jack and Jill are better off sticking with their employer schemes by £449 a year. Even though they would get a £2,000 top-up on the Government scheme, it is not enough to outweigh the higher-rate tax relief of £2,449 they enjoy on the employer schemes.

They also receive child benefit of £3,146 a year (2013/14 rates) for their four children. Under the Government scheme, they would start to lose this as soon as either of them earns over £50,000.

This is a somewhat extreme example, but it illustrates a guiding principle in deciding which scheme to use. If you plan to spend much on childcare for school-age children post autumn 2015, think very carefully before coming out of your employer's scheme.

Unless they put the age limit up, and quickly, it will simply not be worth switching to the new Government scheme.

Employee Shareholders

From 1 September 2013, companies are allowed to offer their staff up to £2,000 of free shares, without any tax or national insurance liability, in exchange for becoming what is officially known as an "employee shareholder".

The company can in fact offer up to £50,000 of free shares to "employee shareholders" although only the first £2,000 will be tax free. The rest will be subject to income tax and national insurance.

Not only that, but the first £50,000 of any gain you make when you ultimately come to sell these shares will be totally exempt from capital gains tax, which is normally payable at 18% or 28%.

Sounds very good so far – but what's the catch? It's all in that phrase "employee shareholder". Apparently that entails giving up certain statutory rights under the Employment Rights Act 1996.

This is the full list of the rights you would be giving up in exchange for your 2,000 pieces of silver:

- Unfair dismissal (apart from automatic reasons)
- Redundancy pay
- To request flexible working arrangements
- To request to undertake a course of study or training

If you take parental or adoption leave, you would also have to give 16 weeks' notice of your intention to return to work, rather than the normal six or eight weeks as the case may be.

For existing employees, any such offer must be optional, but for new employees it can be made mandatory. If the applicant refuses to be an employee shareholder, the employer can simply withdraw the job offer.

However, the employee must be given a seven-day "cooling-off period" during which they can withdraw their acceptance. They must also receive independent legal advice, which the employer must pay for whether the applicant accepts their job offer or not.

You will be pleased to know that existing employees must not be penalised for refusing to be employee shareholders, and any dismissal for this reason will automatically be deemed unfair.

You will also still be protected by The Equality Act and by Health and Safety laws if you do agree to become an employee shareholder, and women will continue to be protected against discrimination if they become pregnant or claim maternity leave.

So what should you do if your employer offers you one of these contracts? The first thing you should do is ask why. Is it just you, or a few other people, or are they being offered to everyone? Much will depend on your own position within the company.

For example, senior executives may welcome these contracts as a way of mitigating tax liabilities on a remuneration package with a significant equity component. Their contracts may well be robust enough not to rely on unfair dismissal or redundancy pay.

However, if your employment contract does not contain robust clauses you should be wary of accepting "employee shareholder" status. Otherwise, you may be first in line for redundancy, or even dismissal, with no legal remedies whatsoever.

Employee shareholders will be protected by the TUPE regulations (Transfer of Undertakings Protection of Employment) in the event of a takeover by another company. However, it has not yet been resolved whether the transferor would be obliged to buy back their shares in that situation, or whether the transferee would be obliged to offer them equivalent shares.

The value of the shares should also be considered carefully. They must be professionally valued for the purpose of these rules and the shares must also be worth having, not a pale shadow of the other share classes in terms of the rights attaching to them.

You should, of course, negotiate hard on the number of shares offered, or on the other terms of your employment contract. For example, you could insist on your statutory rights being replaced by contractual rights against wrongful dismissal or redundancy.

The other thing to think about is tax. Any shares worth more than £2,000 will come with an immediate tax liability, and if you cannot sell the shares yet you will have to find this money somewhere else, possibly from an employer loan.

Finally, you need to consider if/when the shares may eventually be sold, how much they may (or may not) grow in value, whether you will be forced to sell them if you leave the company and how their value will be determined in that event.

National Insurance Employment Allowance

This one is mainly for the bosses. From the 2014/15 tax year, every employer in the country will be entitled to a discount of up to £2,000 on their secondary national insurance contributions. This will be allowed by simple deduction from their PAYE bills.

The good news is that ALL employers will benefit from this allowance. They have managed not to strangle it at birth by tying it up in red tape and excluding certain regions, as happened with the ill-fated national insurance holiday in 2010.

Unless you work for a very small employer, it is unlikely that you will benefit from this new initiative. It is really designed to encourage small firms to take on more staff, not to reward their existing employees or save employers money.

You could argue that employer's national insurance is a tax on jobs and really it is the employee who pays it as otherwise the employer could afford to pay them more. If your boss has a good sense of humour, this could induce him to share the benefits!

On the other hand, he might just tell you to "bog off".

However, the new allowance may well benefit people who hire nannies and other domestic staff. Effectively, they will pay no employer's national insurance on gross wages of more than £22,000 per annum and save them up to £2,000 a year.

The other group who may benefit are contractors working through their own personal service companies. Assuming they can avoid the IR35 tax rules, normal practice is to take a very small salary and large dividends, as then there are no PAYE bills.

For 2013/14 the most tax efficient salary is £7,696 per annum as this avoids national insurance contributions. For 2014/15 they can take a salary of up to £10,000 a year – the level of the income tax personal allowance. This will save them an extra £160 or so.

Pretty small beer, but as Tesco always tell us, every little helps!

Tax-Free Loans

This is a useful measure. They have finally got round to increasing the threshold for tax-free employer loans.

This has been frozen at £5,000 since 1994/95, which was more than enough to buy a car back then, pay for home improvements and fund your annual season ticket. Nowadays, it probably wouldn't even pay for the season ticket.

From 6 April 2014 the threshold is going up to £10,000. As long as you do not exceed this limit for more than a month during the tax year (on ALL loans) you'll pay no tax on an interest-free loan.

At the rate train fares are going up, this is a welcome change. However, you must be under an obligation to actually repay the loan at some point or else it would be treated as taxable income.

If an employer loan exceeds £10,000 the beneficial loan rules will kick in. This means that you must pay interest at a certain rate (4% at present) to avoid a taxable benefit.

This new threshold will be very handy for contractors working through their own personal service companies, as they will have a bit more leeway on their loan account. This keeps track of the difference between their salary/dividends and cash withdrawn.

Medical Interventions

This is a proposal to allow employers to pay up to £500 towards health costs for employees who are on long-term sick leave, in an effort to help them back to work, without a taxable benefit arising.

It is still under consultation at the time of writing and legislation will not be introduced until 2014. However, the proposal is that health measures will be recommended by the new and independent Health and Work Assessment and Advisory Service.

The idea is to get people on long-term sick leave back to work. It will not be compulsory for employers to pay for your health costs, but for those that do, up to £500 will be tax free.

This could enable employers to pay bills from osteopaths and other health professionals without having to report them as taxable benefits on the employee's P11D.

Of course, the medical interventions must be recommended by the new body in order to be tax free. You cannot just come up with your own treatments and get tax-free contributions from your employer towards them.

However, anyone who has been off sick for at least four weeks will have access to occupational health support from the new body. We can only hope it is not overwhelmed by the flood of enquiries.

Employee Share Schemes

There has been a major review of employee share schemes and the following changes were made in the 2013 Finance Act.

Share Incentive Plans

- From 17 July 2013, SIP shares may be issued to employees who have a "material interest" in a close company of 25% or more.

- From 17 July 2013, employers will be able to award shares in a SIP which are subject to restrictions, but the value of those shares for tax purposes must ignore those restrictions.

- From 17 July 2013, employers will be able to apply their own definition of retirement for the "good leaver" provisions (which affects whether or not SIP shares must be forfeited).

- From 17 July 2013, tax relief will be available where shares are withdrawn from a SIP on acceptance of a cash takeover, as long as there was no alternative offer of shares or loan notes.

- From 6 April 2013, there is no longer a £1,500 limit on the value of dividends that can be re-invested in the SIP for the purpose of acquiring dividend shares.

- From 6 April 2013, there is no longer a three-year limit on the time that dividends can be held by SIP trustees without re-investing them in dividend shares.

SAYE Options

- From 11 December 2012, SAYE participants can continue to pay into their plans whilst on sabbatical leave or on secondment to another job in the same organisation.

- From 23 July 2013, it will no longer be possible for employers to offer seven-year SAYE options.

- From 17 July 2013, SAYE options may be issued to employees who have a "material interest" of 25% or more.

- From 17 July 2013, employers will be able to apply their own definition of retirement for the "good leaver" provisions (which affects whether or not SAYE options must be forfeited).

- From 17 July 2013, tax relief will be allowed on the exercise of all SAYE options granted within the previous three years if this is due to a business transfer subject to the TUPE regulations, provided it takes place within six months of the transfer.

- From 17 July 2013, tax relief will be allowed on the exercise of all SAYE options granted within the previous three years if this is required by the terms of a cash takeover, provided there was no opportunity to exchange them for new options in the acquiring company within six months of the offer.

- From 17 July 2013, employers will be able to award SAYE options over shares that are subject to restrictions, but the value of those shares for tax purposes must ignore those restrictions.

Company Share Option Plans

- From 17 July 2013, employers will be able to apply their own definition of retirement for the "good leaver" provisions (which affects whether or not CSOP options must be forfeited).

- From 17 July 2013, tax relief will be allowed on the exercise of all CSOP options granted within the previous three years if this is due to a business transfer subject to the TUPE regulations, provided it takes place within six months of the transfer.

- From 17 July 2013, the definition of a "material interest" in a close company for CSOP options increased from 25% to 30%.

- From 17 July 2013, tax relief will be allowed on the exercise of all CSOP options granted within the previous three years if this is required by the terms of a cash takeover, provided there was no opportunity to exchange them for new options in the acquiring company within six months of the offer.

- From 17 July 2013 employers will be able to award CSOP options over shares that are subject to restrictions, but the value of those shares for tax purposes must ignore those restrictions.

EMI Options

- From 17 July 2013 the period during which an EMI option can be exercised after a "disqualifying event" without losing tax relief is extended from 40 to 90 days.

- From 6 April 2013, Entrepreneurs Relief is allowed on all disposals of shares acquired through EMI options even if the individual does not hold 5% of the ordinary share capital. Also, the usual 12-month minimum holding period is deemed to run from the date of grant.

Summary

Broadly, these changes serve to extend the circumstances in which tax relief is available on employee share schemes. Potentially, the most valuable one is the availability of Entrepreneurs Relief on shares acquired through EMI options.

This reduces the capital gains tax rate from a maximum 28% to just 10% on the eventual disposal of those shares. However, there is no capital gains tax on the exercise of EMI options anyway, so it is only advantageous if you hold on to the shares afterwards.

That would normally only occur if you had to exercise the options before a market existed for the shares because the 10-year deadline was about to expire. Usually, EMI options would only be exercised when the company was about to float or be taken over.

However, notwithstanding this, the most important change for most people is undoubtedly the availability of tax relief where SAYE or CSOP options are exercised within three years following a cash takeover or a business transfer.

This is a very sensible measure as obviously these events are beyond the control of most people and it is only right that they should keep the tax advantages of the scheme. A similar provision applies to Share Incentive Plans where there is a cash takeover.

Lightning Source UK Ltd.
Milton Keynes UK
UKOW03f1449160114

224727UK00001B/11/P